Daily Healthy Salads Cookbook

The Complete Salads Cookbook, featuring tasty salads, with vegetarian, vegan, fish and meat options.

Danielle Harper Smith

Copyright © 2023 Danielle Harper Smith

All rights reserved.

ISBN: 9798872355328

Published by the @dailyhealthysalads Instagram account.

ACKNOWLEDGMENTS

Hello, fellow salad enthusiasts!

As the creator and curator of the @dailyhealthysalads Instagram community, I've had the joy and privilege of connecting with many of you – a vibrant group of individuals who share a passion for health and nutrition. Your enthusiasm, support, and endless curiosity about what goes into our bowls have been the driving force behind this journey.

In our community, we've always believed that eating healthy doesn't mean sacrificing flavor. This cookbook is a testament to that belief. It's filled with recipes that prove healthy eating can be both delicious and satisfying, designed to keep you on track with nutritious and mouth-watering options. Whether you're a long-time health enthusiast or just starting your journey, these recipes are crafted with love, keeping everyone in mind.

A special note about the salads in this book: each recipe is meant for one serving. However, they can easily be scaled up to accommodate more people. Simply adjust the quantities accordingly, and you can enjoy these wholesome salads with friends, family, or whoever might be sharing your table. This flexibility allows everyone to partake in the joy of healthy eating, regardless of the size of your gathering.

I owe a huge thanks to each of you in our @dailyhealthysalads community. Your engagement, feedback, and stories have not only inspired this book but have also made it a reality. This cookbook is as much yours as it is mine.

If you enjoy these recipes as much as I've enjoyed creating them, I'd be thrilled if you could share your experiences. Head over to our Instagram page @dailyhealthysalads to join in on the conversation, share your creations, and, if you're feeling generous, drop a lovely review on Amazon to help spread the word.

Here's to many more delicious, healthy meals together!

With gratitude and greens,
Danielle Harper Smith (a.k.a. Daily Healthy Salads)

CONTENTS

1 Fish Salads   7
2 Meat Salads   47
3 Vegetarian Salads   89
4 Vegan Salads   173

Fish Salads

Spicy Shrimp with Peach and Avocado Salad

Time: 30 mins

Ingredients:
- 4-6 ounces cooked shrimps, peeled and deveined
- 1/2 ripe avocado, diced
- 1/2 ripe peach, diced
- 1/4 cup red bell pepper, diced
- 1/4 cup red onion, finely chopped
- 1/4 cup fresh cilantro, chopped
- 1/2 jalapeño, seeded and finely chopped

Dressing:
- 1 tablespoon olive oil
- 1/2 tablespoon lime juice
- 1/2 teaspoon honey
- 1/2 garlic clove, minced
- Salt and pepper, to taste

Instructions:
1. In a large mixing bowl, combine the cooked shrimp, diced avocado, diced peach, diced red bell pepper, and chopped red onion.
2. Add the chopped cilantro and jalapeño to the bowl.
3. In a separate small bowl, whisk together olive oil, lime juice, honey, and minced garlic to make the dressing. Season with salt and pepper to your liking.
4. Pour the dressing over the shrimp and fruit mixture. Toss gently to coat everything evenly.
5. Taste and adjust seasoning with additional salt and pepper if needed.
6. Serve the salad chilled or at room temperature, garnished with extra cilantro if desired.

Salmon Poke Bowl with Wasabi Mayonnaise

Time: 20 mins

Ingredients:
- 1/4 cup sushi rice, cooked and cooled
- 4-6 ounces sushi-grade salmon, cubed
- 1/2 avocado, sliced
- 2 tablespoons edamame, shelled and cooked
- 1 tablespoon pickled ginger
- 1 tablespoon shredded carrots
- 1/2 cucumber, thinly sliced
- 2 tablespoons green onions, chopped
- 1/2 teaspoon sesame seeds
- 1/2 teaspoon nori strips or seaweed salad (optional)

Dressing:
- 1 tablespoon mayonnaise
- 1 teaspoon wasabi paste (adjust to taste)
- 1 teaspoon soy sauce
- 1/2 teaspoon sesame oil
- 1/2 teaspoon lemon juice

Instructions:
1. Place the cooked sushi rice in the bottom of a bowl.
2. Arrange the salmon, avocado slices, edamame, pickled ginger, shredded carrots, cucumber slices, and nori strips (if using) on top of the rice.
3. In a small bowl, mix together the mayonnaise, wasabi paste, soy sauce, sesame oil, and lemon juice to create the wasabi mayonnaise.
4. Drizzle the wasabi mayonnaise over the ingredients in the bowl.
5. Garnish with chopped green onions and sesame seeds.

Beetroot and Grilled Mackerel Salad

Time: 45 mins

Ingredients:
- 1 medium beetroot, roasted, peeled, and sliced
- 1 mackerel fillet, grilled (approximately 4-6 oz)
- A handful of mixed salad greens
- 2 tablespoons pecans, toasted and roughly chopped
- Fresh herbs (like dill or parsley), for garnish
- Lemon wedges, for serving

Dressing:
- 1 tablespoon extra virgin olive oil
- 1/2 tablespoon lemon juice
- 1/2 teaspoon mustard
- 1/2 teaspoon honey
- Salt and freshly ground black pepper, to taste

Instructions:
1. Preheat the oven to 400°F (200°C). Wrap the beetroots in foil and roast until tender, about 30-40 minutes. Once cooled, peel and slice.
2. Season the mackerel fillets with salt and pepper, and grill them skin-side down until cooked through and the skin is crispy, about 4-6 minutes each side.
3. Prepare the dressing by whisking together olive oil, lemon juice, mustard, honey, salt, and black pepper in a small bowl.
4. Arrange the mixed salad greens on a plate and layer the sliced beetroots on top.
5. Place the grilled mackerel fillets on the salad.
6. Sprinkle with toasted pecans and garnish with fresh herbs.
7. Drizzle the dressing over the salad just before serving.
8. Serve with lemon wedges on the side.

Blackened Fish Taco Salad

Time: 25 mins

Ingredients:
- 4-6 ounces blackened fish fillet, cooked and flaked
- 2 cups shredded romaine lettuce
- 1/2 cup cherry tomatoes, quartered
- 1/2 cup canned black beans, rinsed and drained
- 1/2 cup sweet corn kernels
- 1/2 cup red onion, thinly sliced
- 1/2 avocado, sliced
- A handful of tortilla chips, broken into large pieces

Dressing:
- 1/2 cup Greek yogurt
- 1 tablespoon taco seasoning
- Juice of 1/2 lime
- Salt to taste

Instructions:
1. Cook the fish fillets with a blackening spice blend until cooked through and easily flaked with a fork. Set aside to cool slightly, then flake into bite-sized pieces.
2. In a large salad bowl, toss the shredded romaine lettuce with cherry tomatoes, black beans, sweet corn, and sliced red onion.
3. Arrange the salad on plates, and top with flaked fish, avocado slices, and tortilla chips.
4. In a small bowl, mix together Greek yogurt, taco seasoning, lime juice, and salt to make the dressing. Adjust the seasoning to taste.
5. Drizzle the dressing over the salads just before serving.
6. Serve immediately, garnished with extra lime wedges if desired.

Chili-Lime Shrimp and Avocado Salad

Time: 20 mins

Ingredients:
- 4-6 ounces shrimps, peeled and deveined
- 1/2 ripe avocado, diced
- 1/2 cup diced mango
- 1/2 cup sweet corn kernels
- A handful of fresh cilantro leaves
- 1 tablespoon red onion, finely chopped
- A pinch of chili flakes (adjust to taste)
- 1 cup mixed salad greens (such as arugula or baby spinach) for base

Dressing:
- Juice of 1 lime
- 1 tablespoon extra-virgin olive oil
- 1/2 teaspoon honey (optional, for a touch of sweetness)
- Salt and pepper to taste

Instructions:
1. Arrange a bed of mixed salad greens on a plate.
2. In a medium bowl, combine the cooked shrimp, diced avocado, mango, corn kernels, and red onion.
3. In a small bowl, whisk together the lime juice, olive oil, honey (if using), and a pinch of salt and pepper until well combined.
4. Drizzle the dressing over the shrimp mixture and toss gently to coat everything evenly.
5. Top the bed of greens with the dressed shrimp mixture.
6. Garnish with fresh cilantro leaves and sprinkle with chili flakes to your desired level of heat.
7. Serve immediately, with additional lime wedges if desired.

Egg, Red Pepper, and Anchovy Salad

Time: 15 mins

Ingredients:
- 2 cups fresh baby spinach leaves
- 1/2 red bell pepper, thinly sliced
- 2 anchovy fillets, chopped (optional)
- 1 tablespoon pine nuts, toasted
- 1 soft-boiled egg, halved
- Freshly ground black pepper to taste

Dressing:
- 2 tablespoons extra virgin olive oil
- 1 tablespoon balsamic vinegar
- 1/2 teaspoon Dijon mustard
- A pinch of salt

Instructions:
1. Arrange the baby spinach as a bed on a serving plate.
2. Scatter the sliced red bell pepper and chopped anchovies (if using) over the spinach.
3. Place the soft-boiled egg halves on top.
4. Sprinkle the toasted pine nuts over the salad.
5. In a small bowl, whisk together the olive oil, balsamic vinegar, Dijon mustard, and a pinch of salt to make the dressing.
6. Drizzle the dressing over the salad.
7. Finish with a generous grind of black pepper.
8. Serve immediately, enjoying the runny yolk mixing with the dressing.

Greek Yogurt Tuna Salad

Time: 15 mins

Ingredients:
- 3-6 ounces tuna in water, drained and flaked
- 1/2 cup Greek yogurt
- 1/2 cup cucumber, diced
- 1/2 cup cherry tomatoes, halved
- 1/2 cup red onion, finely chopped

Dressing:
- Fresh dill, chopped, to taste
- A pinch of salt
- Black pepper to taste

Instructions:
1. In a mixing bowl, combine the flaked tuna and Greek yogurt, stirring until the tuna is well coated.
2. Add the diced cucumber, halved cherry tomatoes, and finely chopped red onion to the bowl.
3. Sprinkle with chopped fresh dill, and season with salt and black pepper to your liking.
4. Gently mix all the ingredients together until everything is evenly distributed.
5. Taste and adjust the seasoning if necessary.
6. The salad can be served immediately or chilled in the refrigerator for 30 minutes to allow the flavors to meld together.
7. Serve as a light lunch or as a side dish with your main meal.

Grilled Prawn and Halloumi Salad

Time: 15 mins

Ingredients:
- 4-6 ounces prawns, peeled and deveined
- 2 slices of halloumi cheese about 1/4 inch thick
- 1/2 cup cherry tomatoes
- 1/2 cucumber, thinly sliced
- 1/2 cup mixed salad leaves
- Fresh parsley for garnish

Dressing:
- 1 tablespoon olive oil
- 1 teaspoon lemon juice
- 1/2 teaspoon honey
- 1/2 teaspoon mustard
- Salt and pepper to taste

Instructions:
1. Season the prawns and halloumi with salt and pepper.
2. Heat a grill pan over medium heat and cook the prawns for 1-2 minutes on each side or until they are pink and cooked through.
3. Grill the halloumi for 1-2 minutes on each side or until there are golden-brown grill marks.
4. In a bowl, whisk together the olive oil, lemon juice, honey, mustard, salt, and pepper to create the dressing
5. Arrange the mixed salad leaves on a plate, top with sliced cucumber, cherry tomatoes, grilled prawns, and halloumi.
6. Drizzle with the dressing and garnish with fresh parsley before serving.

Roasted Salmon Salad with Lemon Vinaigrette

Time: 25 mins

Ingredients:
- 1 salmon fillet (approximately 4 oz)
- 1/2 cup asparagus, trimmed
- 1/4 cup cherry tomatoes, halved
- 1/4 of red onion, thinly sliced
- 1 cup mixed greens (such as arugula and spinach)
- Olive oil for cooking

Dressing:
- 1 tablespoon extra virgin olive oil
- 1/2 teaspoon fresh lemon juice
- 1/2 teaspoon honey
- 1/2 teaspoon Dijon mustard
- Salt and freshly ground black pepper to taste

Instructions:
1. Preheat the oven to 400°F (200°C).
2. Season the salmon fillet with salt and pepper and drizzle with olive oil.
3. Place the salmon on a baking sheet and roast in the oven for about 12-15 minutes, or until cooked through.
4. While the salmon is cooking, blanch the asparagus in boiling water for 2-3 minutes until tender but still crisp.
5. To make the dressing, whisk together the olive oil, lemon juice, honey, Dijon mustard, salt, and pepper in a small bowl.
6. Arrange the mixed greens on a plate and top with the blanched asparagus, cherry tomatoes, and red onion.
7. Once the salmon is cooked, place it on top of the salad.
8. Drizzle the lemon vinaigrette over the salad and salmon.

Smoked Mackerel with Potatoes and Horseradish Salad

Time: 35 mins

Ingredients:
- 3-6 ounces smoked mackerel fillet
- 1/4 cup new potatoes
- 1/4 cup fresh watercress
- 1/4 cup fresh parsley, chopped
- 1/4 cup fresh chives, chopped
- 1/4 cup small capers

Dressing:
- 1 tablespoon crème fraîche
- 1/2 teaspoon prepared horseradish
- 1/2 teaspoon Dijon mustard
- 1/2 teaspoon lemon juice
- Salt and pepper, to taste

Instructions:
1. Boil the potatoes in salted water until tender, about 15-20 minutes. Drain and let them cool slightly.
2. While the potatoes are still warm, cut them into halves or quarters, depending on size.
3. Flake the smoked mackerel fillet into bite-sized pieces.
4. In a small bowl, mix together crème fraîche, horseradish, Dijon mustard, and lemon juice. Season with salt and pepper to taste.
5. In a mixing bowl, gently toss the warm potatoes, cooked green peas, watercress, parsley, and chives with half of the dressing.
6. Arrange the salad on a plate and top with flaked mackerel.
7. Drizzle the remaining dressing over the mackerel and season with additional salt and pepper if needed.
8. Serve the salad warm with extra herbs sprinkled on top.

Grilled Romaine Lettuce and Prawns Salad

Time: 20 mins

Ingredients:
- 4-6 ounces prawns, peeled and deveined
- 1/2 head of romaine lettuce, halved lengthwise
- 1 tablespoon olive oil
- Salt and pepper to taste
- 1 tablespoon grated parmesan cheese
- Lemon wedges for serving

Dressing:
- 3 tablespoons olive oil
- 1 tablespoon lemon juice
- 1 teaspoon Dijon mustard
- 1/2 garlic clove, minced
- 1/2 teaspoon Worcestershire sauce
- Salt and pepper to taste

Instructions:
1. Preheat the grill to medium-high heat.
2. Brush the prawns and romaine lettuce with olive oil and season with salt and pepper.
3. Grill the prawns for 2-3 minutes on each side until they turn pink and are cooked through.
4. Place the romaine lettuce cut side down on the grill and cook for about 2 minutes until the lettuce is slightly charred and wilting.
5. In a small bowl, whisk together the ingredients for the dressing until emulsified.
6. Arrange the grilled romaine lettuce on plates and top with the prawns
7. Drizzle with the dressing and sprinkle with parmesan cheese.
8. Serve with lemon wedges on the side.

Salmon, Peas, and Brown Rice Salad

Time: 30 mins

Ingredients:
- 1 salmon fillet (approximately 4 oz)
- 1/2 cup cooked brown rice, cooled
- 1/4 cup fresh peas, blanched
- 1/2 cup baby spinach leaves
- Fresh dill for garnish
- Lemon wedges for serving
- Salt and pepper to taste

Dressing:
- 1 tablespoon extra virgin olive oil
- 1/2 tablespoon lemon juice
- 1/2 teaspoon Dijon mustard
- 1/2 teaspoon honey
- Salt and freshly ground black pepper to taste

Instructions:
1. If the salmon is not precooked, season the fillet with salt and pepper, and cook it in a preheated pan over medium heat, or bake at 375°F (190°C) for 12-15 minutes until cooked through.
2. In a bowl, mix the cooked brown rice with the blanched peas and baby spinach leaves.
3. Prepare the dressing by whisking together the olive oil, lemon juice, Dijon mustard, honey, salt, and pepper in a small bowl.
4. Place the rice mixture on a plate as a bed for the salad.
5. Once the salmon is cooked, place it on top of the rice mixture.
6. Drizzle the dressing over the salmon and salad.
7. Garnish with fresh dill and serve with lemon wedges on the side.

Grilled Shrimps with Grapefruit and Avocado Salad

Time: 20 mins

Ingredients:
- 4-6 ounces shrimps, peeled and deveined
- 1/2 avocado, sliced
- 1/2 grapefruit, peeled and sections cut out
- 1/4 cup radishes, thinly sliced
- 1/4 cup red onion, thinly sliced
- 2 tablespoons feta cheese, crumbled
- Fresh cilantro for garnish
- Salt and pepper to taste

Dressing:
- 2 tablespoons olive oil
- 1 tablespoon grapefruit juice (from remaining grapefruit)
- 1 teaspoon honey
- 1/2 teaspoon apple cider vinegar
- Salt and pepper to taste

Instructions:
1. Season the shrimp with salt and pepper.
2. Heat a grill pan over medium-high heat and cook the shrimp for 2 minutes on each side or until they are pink and cooked through.
3. In a small bowl, whisk together the olive oil, grapefruit juice, honey, apple cider vinegar, salt, and pepper to create the dressing.
4. Arrange the avocado slices and grapefruit sections on a plate.
5. Top with grilled shrimp, sliced radishes, and red onion.
6. Sprinkle with crumbled feta cheese and garnish with fresh cilantro.
7. Drizzle with the dressing before serving.

Smoked Salmon and Blood Orange Salad

Time: 15 mins

Ingredients:
- 4-6 ounces smoked salmon, sliced
- 1 blood orange, peeled and segments cut out
- 1 tablespoon pomegranate seeds
- 1 tablespoon pumpkin seeds, toasted
- 1/4 cup kale leaves, stems removed and chopped
- 1/2 tablespoon olive oil
- Salt and pepper, to taste

Dressing:
- 1 tablespoon extra virgin olive oil
- 1/2 teaspoon honey
- 1/2 teaspoon apple cider vinegar
- Salt and pepper, to taste

Instructions:
1. Spread the chopped kale leaves on a serving plate as a bed for the salad.
2. Arrange the smoked salmon slices and blood orange segments on top of the kale.
3. Sprinkle pomegranate seeds and toasted pumpkin seeds over the salmon and oranges.
4. In a small bowl, whisk together the extra virgin olive oil, honey, and apple cider vinegar. Season with salt and pepper to taste.
5. Drizzle the dressing generously over the salad just before serving.
6. Serve immediately, offering additional dressing on the side if desired.

Smoked Salmon and Egg Salad with Caper Dressing

Time: 20 mins

Ingredients:
- 4 ounces smoked salmon, sliced
- 1 handful mixed greens (spinach, arugula, etc.)
- 1 hard-boiled egg, halved
- 1/2 tablespoons capers
- 1/2 tablespoon fresh dill, chopped
- Salt and pepper, to taste

Dressing:
- 1 tablespoon extra virgin olive oil
- 1/2 tablespoon lemon juice
- 1/2 teaspoon Dijon mustard
- 1/2 teaspoon honey
- 1/2 tablespoon capers, finely chopped
- Salt and pepper, to taste

Instructions:
1. Arrange mixed greens on a serving plate.
2. Drape slices of smoked salmon over the greens.
3. Place the hard-boiled egg halves on the salad.
4. Sprinkle capers and fresh dill over the top.
5. In a small bowl, whisk together the olive oil, lemon juice, Dijon mustard, honey, and chopped capers for the dressing. Season with salt and pepper.
6. Drizzle the dressing over the salad just before serving.
7. Serve immediately with additional seasoning if needed.

Som Tam (Papaya Salad)

Time: 20 mins

Ingredients:
- 1 small green papaya, shredded
- 4-5 ounces cooked prawns, peeled
- 1/2 cup cherry tomatoes, halved
- 1/4 cup bean sprouts
- 1/4 cup carrots, julienned
- 1 tablespoon roasted peanuts, crushed
- 1 tablespoon fresh cilantro leaves
- Salt, to taste

Dressing:
- 1/2 tablespoon fresh lime juice
- 1/2 tablespoon fish sauce
- 1/2 teaspoon palm sugar, grated
- 1/2 garlic clove, minced
- 1 small chili, sliced
- Adjust salt as per taste

Instructions:
1. In a large mortar, pound garlic and chili to a paste.
2. Add palm sugar, fish sauce, and lime juice, and mix until the sugar dissolves.
3. Add the shredded green papaya, carrots, and cherry tomatoes to the mortar (or mixing bowl if preferred).
4. Mix and pound gently with the pestle, allowing the flavors to combine and vegetables to bruise lightly.
5. Toss in the cooked prawns and bean sprouts, and give it a light mix.
6. Transfer the salad to a serving plate, sprinkle with crushed peanuts and cilantro leaves.
7. Serve immediately, with additional lime wedges if desired.

Thai Prawn Noodle Salad with Peanut Dressing

Time: 20 mins

Ingredients:
- 1/4 cup rice noodles
- 4-6 ounces cooked prawns (shrimp)
- 1/4 red bell pepper, thinly sliced
- 1/4 carrot, julienned
- 1 spring onion, thinly sliced
- 1 tablespoon chopped peanuts
- Fresh cilantro, for garnish
- Lime wedge, for serving

Dressing:
- 1 tablespoon peanut butter
- 1/2 tablespoon soy sauce
- 1/2 tablespoon lime juice
- 1/2 teaspoon honey
- 1/2 teaspoon grated ginger
- 1/2 teaspoon crushed garlic
- A pinch of chili flakes (optional)

Instructions:
1. Prepare the rice noodles according to package instructions. Drain and set aside.
2. For the dressing, whisk together peanut butter, soy sauce, lime juice, honey, ginger, garlic, and water in a small bowl. Adjust the consistency with more water if necessary. Add chili flakes if desired.
3. In a serving bowl, combine the rice noodles, prawns, red bell pepper, carrot, and spring onion.
4. Drizzle the peanut dressing over the salad and toss to combine everything evenly.
5. Garnish with chopped peanuts, fresh coriander leaves, and a wedge of lime on the side.

Tuna, Avocado, and Chickpeas Salad

Time: 15 mins

Ingredients:
- 1 cup mixed salad greens (arugula and spinach)
- 3-6 ounces tuna, drained and flaked
- 1/2 cup chickpeas, drained and rinsed
- 1/2 avocado, sliced
- 1/4 cup sliced cucumber
- 1/4 cup pickled red onion
- Fresh parsley, chopped (for garnish)

Dressing:
- 2 tablespoons extra virgin olive oil
- 1 tablespoon lemon juice
- 1/2 teaspoon honey
- 1/4 teaspoon Dijon mustard
- Salt and pepper to taste

Instructions:
1. Arrange the mixed salad greens at the bottom of a serving bowl.
2. Add the flaked tuna, chickpeas, sliced cucumber, and pickled red onion on top of the greens.
3. Neatly place the sliced avocado on one side of the bowl.
4. To make the dressing, whisk together the olive oil, lemon juice, honey, Dijon mustard, salt, and pepper in a small bowl until the mixture is well blended.
5. Drizzle the dressing over the salad.
6. Garnish with chopped fresh parsley.
7. Serve immediately and savor your Tuna, Avocado, and Chickpea Salad!

Tuna Niçoise Salad

Time: 20 mins

Ingredients:
- 1 cup mixed salad greens
- 3-6 ounces tuna in olive oil, flaked
- 1 hard-boiled eggs, quartered
- 1/2 cup cherry tomatoes, halved
- 1 tablespoon black olives
- 1/2 cup pickled cucumbers, sliced
- 1/4 red onion, thinly sliced
- Fresh herbs (parsley or dill), for garnish

Dressing:
- 3 tablespoons extra virgin olive oil
- 1 teaspoon red wine vinegar
- 1/2 teaspoon Dijon mustard
- 1/2 small garlic clove, minced
- Salt and pepper to taste

Instructions:
1. Arrange the mixed salad greens on a large plate.
2. Top the greens with flaked tuna, quartered hard-boiled eggs, halved cherry tomatoes, black olives, and sliced cucumbers.
3. Scatter the thinly sliced red onion and fresh herbs over the salad.
4. For the dressing, whisk together the olive oil, red wine vinegar, Dijon mustard, minced garlic, salt, and pepper in a small bowl until well combined.
5. Drizzle the dressing over the salad just before serving.

Meat Salads

Asian-Style Ginger Pork Salad

Time: 35 mins

Ingredients:
- 3-4 ounces pork tenderloin, thinly sliced
- 1 cup red cabbage, shredded
- 1/2 tablespoon honey and soy sauce
- 1/2 garlic clove, minced
- 1 tablespoon vegetable oil
- 1 teaspoon sesame seeds
- Fresh cilantro and sliced green onions for garnish

Dressing:
- 1 tablespoon soy sauce
- 1/2 tablespoon rice vinegar
- 1/2 tablespoon sesame oil
- 1/2 teaspoon honey
- 1/2 teaspoon fresh ginger, grated
- 1/2 garlic clove, minced
- Chili flakes to taste (optional)

Instructions:
1. Mix soy sauce, honey, grated ginger, and minced garlic in a bowl; marinate pork slices in this mixture for at least 15 minutes.
2. Cook the marinated pork in vegetable oil in a pan over medium-high heat until browned; season with salt and pepper.
3. Lay shredded red cabbage in a large bowl to create a bed for the pork.
4. Place the cooked pork slices on top of the red cabbage.
5. Garnish the pork with sesame seeds, cilantro leaves, and sliced green onions; drizzle with a dressing made from soy sauce, rice vinegar, sesame oil, honey, ginger, garlic, and chili flakes before serving.

BLT Salad

Time: 20 mins

Ingredients:
- 1 cup chopped romaine lettuce
- 2 slices of bacon, cooked and chopped (approximately 2 oz)
- 1/2 cup cherry tomatoes, halved
- 1/2 cup croutons
- Optional: Sliced turkey breast for a twist on the traditional BLT

Dressing:
- 1/2 cup mayonnaise
- 1/2 tablespoon milk (to thin the dressing)
- 1/2 teaspoon dried parsley
- 1/2 teaspoon garlic powder
- Salt and freshly ground black pepper, to taste

Instructions:
1. Cook the bacon in a skillet over medium heat until crispy. Once cooked, place on paper towels to drain, then chop into bite-sized pieces.
2. In a large mixing bowl, combine the chopped romaine lettuce with the halved cherry tomatoes and croutons.
3. If you're adding turkey, layer thinly sliced turkey breast onto the salad.
4. In a small bowl, whisk together the mayonnaise, milk, dried parsley, garlic powder, salt, and pepper to create the dressing.
5. Drizzle the dressing over the salad and toss gently to coat all the ingredients.
6. Top the salad with the chopped bacon.
7. Serve immediately, ensuring the bacon remains crisp.

Chicken, Avocado, and Strawberry Spinach Salad

Time: 30 mins

Ingredients:
- 4-6 ounces grilled chicken breast, sliced
- 1 cup fresh spinach leaves
- 1/2 avocado, sliced
- 1/2 cup strawberries, sliced
- 2 tablespoons red onion, thinly sliced
- 1 tablespoon feta cheese, crumbled

Dressing:
- 2 tablespoons balsamic vinaigrette

Instructions:
1. Grill the chicken breast seasoned with salt and pepper over medium heat until it reaches an internal temperature of 165°F (74°C), about 5 minutes on each side. Let it rest for a few minutes before slicing.
2. Rinse the spinach leaves and pat them dry. Place them in a large salad bowl.
3. Add the sliced strawberries, avocado, and red onion to the spinach.
4. Slice the rested chicken and arrange it on top of the salad.
5. Sprinkle the crumbled feta cheese over the salad.
6. Drizzle with balsamic vinaigrette just before serving.
7. Toss lightly to combine when ready to eat.
8. Serve this delightful combination of savory chicken, creamy avocado, sweet strawberries, and tangy feta cheese for a refreshing and satisfying meal.

Chicken Caesar Salad

Time: 30 mins

Ingredients:
- 4-6 ounces grilled chicken breast, sliced
- 1 cup romaine lettuce, torn into pieces
- 1/2 cup croutons
- 2 tablespoons shaved Parmesan cheese
- Lemon wedge for garnish

Dressing:
- 2 tablespoons Caesar dressing (store-bought or homemade)

Instructions:
1. If starting with raw chicken, season the chicken breast with salt and pepper. Grill over medium heat for about 5 minutes on each side or until the internal temperature reaches 165°F (74°C). Allow it to rest for a few minutes before slicing.
2. Wash and dry the romaine lettuce leaves, then tear them into bite-sized pieces.
3. In a large bowl, combine the lettuce, croutons, and sliced chicken.
4. Drizzle Caesar dressing over the salad and toss gently to coat all the ingredients.
5. Transfer the salad to a serving plate.
6. Top with shaved Parmesan cheese.
7. Serve with a lemon wedge on the side.
8. Enjoy this classic and satisfying salad as a meal on its own or as a side dish.

Chicken Satay Salad

Time: 35 mins

Ingredients:
- 4-6 ounces grilled chicken breast, sliced (marinated in satay sauce)
- 1 cup mixed greens (lettuce, spinach)
- 1/2 cup cucumber, thinly sliced
- 1/2 cup carrots, julienned
- 1/2 cup bell peppers, thinly sliced
- 1/2 tablespoon peanuts, crushed
- Fresh cilantro for garnish

Dressing:
- 1 tablespoon satay sauce (store-bought or homemade)
- 1/2 tablespoon peanut butter
- 1/2 teaspoon soy sauce
- 1/2 teaspoon honey
- 1/2 teaspoon lime juice
- Water to thin, if needed

Instructions:
1. Marinate the chicken breast in satay sauce for at least 30 minutes, then grill over medium heat for about 5 minutes on each side or until fully cooked. Allow it to rest before slicing.
2. Prepare the mixed greens and vegetables and arrange them on a serving plate.
3. In a small bowl, whisk together the satay sauce, peanut butter, soy sauce, honey, and lime juice until smooth. If the dressing is too thick, add a little water to reach the desired consistency.
4. Place the grilled chicken slices on top of the salad greens.
5. Drizzle the dressing over the salad and chicken.
6. Garnish with crushed peanuts and fresh cilantro.

Cobb Salad with Grilled Chicken

Time: 30 mins

Ingredients:
- 4-6 ounces boneless, skinless chicken breast
- 1 cup romaine lettuce, chopped
- 1/2 ripe avocado, sliced
- 1/2 cup cherry tomatoes, halved
- 1/2 cup crumbled blue cheese
- 2 slices bacon, cooked and crumbled
- 1 hard-boiled egg, sliced
- Salt and pepper to taste

Dressing:
- 2 tablespoons olive oil
- 1 tablespoon red wine vinegar
- 1 teaspoon Dijon mustard
- 1/2 teaspoon honey
- A pinch of garlic powder
- Salt and pepper to taste

Instructions:
1. Season the chicken breast with salt and pepper and grill over medium heat for about 6-7 minutes on each side, until the internal temperature reaches 165°F (74°C). Let it rest for a few minutes before slicing.
2. Arrange the chopped romaine lettuce as the base on a plate.
3. Neatly place the sliced chicken, avocado, tomatoes, crumbled blue cheese, bacon, and egg on top of the lettuce in rows.
4. In a small bowl, whisk together the olive oil, red wine vinegar, Dijon mustard, honey, garlic powder, and a pinch of salt and pepper to create the dressing.
5. Drizzle the dressing over the salad just before serving.

Greek Marinated Chicken Gyro Salad

Time: 1 hour and 10 mins

Ingredients:
- 4-6 ounces chicken breast, grilled and sliced
- 1 cup lettuce, chopped
- 1/2 cup cherry tomatoes, halved
- 1/2 cup cucumber, sliced
- 1/2 cup red onion, thinly sliced
- 1/2 cup Kalamata olives
- 2 tablespoons feta cheese, crumbled
- 1/2 avocado, sliced
- Salt to taste
- Black pepper to taste

Chicken Marinade:
- 2 tablespoons olive oil
- 1 tablespoon lemon juice
- 1/2 garlic clove, minced
- 1/2 teaspoon dried oregano
- Salt and pepper to taste

Dressing:
- 3 tablespoons olive oil
- 1 tablespoon red wine vinegar
- 1/2 teaspoon dried oregano
- 1/2 teaspoon garlic powder
- Salt and pepper to taste

Instructions:
1. In a bowl, whisk together the olive oil, lemon juice, minced garlic, dried oregano, salt, and pepper. Marinate the chicken in this mixture for at least 30 minutes in the refrigerator.
2. Grill the chicken over medium heat until cooked through and nicely charred. Let it rest before slicing.
3. In a large salad bowl, combine the chopped lettuce, halved cherry tomatoes, sliced cucumber, thinly sliced red onion, and Kalamata olives.
4. Top the salad with the grilled, sliced chicken and crumbled feta cheese.
5. Arrange the avocado slices around the salad.
6. For the dressing, whisk together olive oil, red wine vinegar, dried oregano, garlic powder, salt, and pepper in a small bowl.
7. Drizzle the dressing over the salad just before serving.

Grilled Chicken, Bok Choy, and Mango Salad

Time: 30 mins

Ingredients:
- 4-6 ounces chicken breast, grilled and sliced
- 1 cup bok choy, steamed and cooled
- 1/2 ripe mango, cubed
- 1 carrot, julienned
- 1 tablespoon fresh cilantro, chopped
- Sesame seeds for garnish
- Salt and pepper to taste

Dressing:
- 1 tablespoon soy sauce
- 1/2 tablespoon honey
- 1/2 tablespoon sesame oil
- 1/2 teaspoon rice vinegar
- 1/2 garlic clove, minced
- 1/2 teaspoon fresh ginger, grated
- Chili flakes to taste (optional)

Instructions:
1. Grill the chicken breast until thoroughly cooked, let it rest, then slice it.
2. Steam the bok choy until it is tender, then let it cool.
3. On a serving plate, arrange the cooled bok choy.
4. Add the julienned carrot and cubed mango around the bok choy.
5. Place the grilled chicken slices on top of the greens.
6. Sprinkle with fresh chopped cilantro and sesame seeds.
7. For the dressing, whisk together soy sauce, honey, sesame oil, rice vinegar, minced garlic, grated ginger, and chili flakes if using in a small bowl.
8. Drizzle the dressing over the salad before serving.
9. Serve the salad with additional dressing on the side if desired.

Larb Salad with Thai Dressing

Time: 1 hour

Ingredients:
- 4-6 ounces ground lamb, cooked
- 1 cup butter lettuce leaves
- 1/2 cup cucumber, thinly sliced
- 1 cup radishes, thinly sliced
- 1 tablespoon red onions, chopped
- Fresh mint leaves for garnish
- Salt and pepper to taste

Dressing:
- 1 tablespoon fish sauce
- 1 teaspoon lime juice
- 1 teaspoon brown sugar
- 1/2 clove garlic, finely minced
- 1 small chili, finely chopped (optional for heat)
- Salt and pepper to taste

Instructions:
1. Cook the ground lamb in a skillet over medium heat until browned. Season with salt and pepper. Set aside to cool.
2. Arrange the butter lettuce leaves on a serving plate.
3. Top the lettuce with the cooked ground lamb, cucumber slices, radish slices, and red onion.
4. To make the dressing, combine fish sauce, lime juice, brown sugar, minced garlic, and chopped chili in a small bowl. Stir until the sugar dissolves.
5. Drizzle the Thai dressing over the salad.
6. Garnish with fresh mint leaves.
7. Serve with a wedge of lime on the side for additional flavor if desired.

Melon, Parma Ham, and Arugula Salad

Time: 10 mins

Ingredients:
- 1 cup arugula leaves
- 3 slices of Parma ham (approximately 3 oz)
- 1 cup melon (cantaloupe or similar), sliced
- Freshly ground black pepper to taste

Dressing:
- 1 tablespoon extra virgin olive oil
- 1 tablespoon balsamic vinegar
- 1 teaspoon honey
- Salt to taste

Instructions:
1. Wash and dry the arugula leaves and arrange them on a serving plate.
2. Drape the slices of Parma ham over the arugula.
3. Scatter the sliced melon around the salad.
4. For the dressing, whisk together the extra virgin olive oil, balsamic vinegar, honey, and salt in a small bowl.
5. Drizzle the dressing over the salad.
6. Finish with freshly ground black pepper over the top to your liking.
7. Serve immediately, preferably chilled.

Mixed Berry and Quinoa Chicken Salad

Time: 30 mins

Ingredients:
- 1/2 cup cooked quinoa
- 1 cup mixed greens (spinach and arugula)
- 4-6 ounces grilled chicken breast, sliced
- 1/4 cup blackberries
- 1/4 cup raspberries
- 1/4 cup blueberries
- 1/4 cup sliced strawberries
- 2 tablespoons red onion, finely chopped
- 1 teaspoon red quinoa, uncooked (for garnish)
- 1 tablespoon green onions, chopped (for garnish)

Dressing:
- 2 tablespoons balsamic vinegar
- 1 tablespoon extra virgin olive oil
- 1 teaspoon honey
- Salt and pepper to taste

Instructions:
1. Cook the quinoa according to the package instructions and let it cool.
2. Grill the chicken breast until fully cooked, let it cool, and slice it.
3. In a large bowl, combine the mixed greens, cooled quinoa, and sliced chicken.
4. Add the blackberries, raspberries, blueberries, and strawberries to the bowl.
5. Sprinkle the finely chopped red onion over the salad.
6. In a small bowl, whisk together the balsamic vinegar, olive oil, honey, salt, and pepper.
7. Pour the dressing over the salad and toss gently to combine.
8. Garnish with uncooked red quinoa and chopped green onions.
9. Serve immediately or chill in the refrigerator for up to an hour before serving.

Mixed Green and Bresaola Salad

Time: 10 mins

Ingredients:
- 1 cup mixed greens (arugula, spinach.)
- 4-6 ounces bresaola, thinly sliced
- 1 small zucchini, ribboned with a peeler
- 1 tablespoon shaved Parmesan cheese
- 1 teaspoon pine nuts (optional)
- Salt and black pepper to taste

Dressing:
- 1 tablespoon extra virgin olive oil
- 1 tablespoon balsamic vinegar
- 1/2 teaspoon Dijon mustard
- 1/2 teaspoon honey
- Salt and pepper to taste

Instructions:
1. Place the mixed greens in a large salad bowl.
2. Arrange the bresaola slices and zucchini ribbons on top of the greens.
3. In a small bowl, whisk together the olive oil, balsamic vinegar, Dijon mustard, honey, salt, and pepper to create the dressing.
4. Drizzle the dressing over the salad and toss lightly to coat.
5. Top with shaved Parmesan and pine nuts if using.
6. Season with a pinch of salt and freshly ground black pepper to taste.
7. Serve immediately as a fresh appetizer or a light meal.

Peachy Prosciutto Burrata Salad

Time: 10 mins

Ingredients:
- 1 ripe nectarine, sliced
- 2 slices of Parma ham (approximately 2 oz)
- 1 small burrata cheese (approximately 2 oz)
- A handful of arugula leaves
- Fresh basil leaves for garnish
- Balsamic glaze for drizzling
- Salt and black pepper to taste

Dressing:
- 1 tablespoon extra virgin olive oil
- 1/2 tablespoon balsamic vinegar
- A pinch of salt
- A crack of black pepper

Instructions:
1. Begin by placing the arugula leaves on a plate as the base of the salad.
2. Tear the prosciutto slices into smaller pieces and scatter them over the arugula.
3. Cut the nectarine into slices, removing the pit, and arrange them around the plate.
4. Place the burrata cheese in the center of the salad.
5. In a small bowl, whisk together the extra virgin olive oil, balsamic vinegar, salt, and pepper to create the dressing.
6. Drizzle the dressing evenly over the salad.
7. Garnish with fresh basil leaves.
8. Finish off with a drizzle of balsamic glaze and a sprinkle of salt and pepper to taste.
9. Serve immediately and enjoy!

Peanut Chicken Soba Noodle Salad

Time: 25 mins

Ingredients:
- 1 cup cooked soba noodles
- 4-6 ounces cooked and shredded chicken breast
- 1/2 cup sliced red bell pepper
- 1/2 cup French beans, chopped and cooked
- 1 tablespoon chopped green onions (scallions)
- 1 tablespoon fresh cilantro leaves
- 1 tablespoon sesame seeds
- 1 tablespoon chopped peanuts

Dressing:
- 1 tablespoon peanut butter
- 1/2 tablespoon soy sauce
- 1/2 tablespoon rice vinegar
- 1/2 tablespoon sesame oil
- 1 teaspoon honey
- 1/2 teaspoon grated ginger
- Water to thin, if necessary

Instructions:
1. Cook the soba noodles according to the package instructions, then rinse under cold water and drain.
2. In a large bowl, combine the soba noodles, shredded chicken, red bell pepper, French beans, green onions, cilantro, sesame seeds, and peanuts.
3. In a small bowl, whisk together the peanut butter, soy sauce, rice vinegar, sesame oil, honey, and grated ginger until smooth. If the dressing is too thick, add a little water to reach the desired consistency.
4. Pour the dressing over the noodle mixture and toss to coat evenly.
5. Garnish with additional sesame seeds and peanuts if desired.
6. Serve chilled or at room temperature.

Pork, Apple, and Blue Cheese Salad

Time: 30 mins

Ingredients:
- 3-4 ounces pork tenderloin, grilled and thinly sliced
- 1 medium apple, cored and thinly sliced
- 2 tablespoons crumbled blue cheese
- 1 tablespoon walnuts, toasted and chopped
- 1 cup mixed salad greens

Dressing:
- 1 tablespoon extra virgin olive oil
- 1/2 tablespoon apple cider vinegar
- 1/2 teaspoon Dijon mustard
- 1/2 teaspoon honey
- Salt and freshly ground black pepper to taste

Instructions:
1. If the pork is not precooked, grill the pork tenderloin over medium heat until it reaches an internal temperature of 145°F (63°C). Let it rest for a few minutes before slicing.
2. Arrange the mixed salad greens on a plate.
3. Layer the sliced pork and apple over the greens.
4. Sprinkle with crumbled blue cheese and toasted walnuts.
5. In a small bowl, whisk together the olive oil, apple cider vinegar, Dijon mustard, honey, salt, and black pepper to create the dressing.
6. Drizzle the dressing over the salad.
7. Serve immediately, pairing with a glass of your favorite wine if desired.

Seared Beef and Pomelo Salad

Time: 25 mins

Ingredients:
- 3-4 ounces beef tenderloin, thinly sliced
- 1/4 cup bean sprouts
- 1 tablespoon fresh coriander leaves
- 1 tablespoon fresh mint leaves
- 1/4 small red onion, thinly sliced
- 1/4 pomelo, peeled and segments removed
- 1/2 small carrot, julienned
- 1/2 tablespoon crushed peanuts
- 1/2 teaspoon sesame seeds
- 1 red chili, thinly sliced
- 1 lime wedge, for garnish

Dressing:
- 1 tablespoon soy sauce
- 1/2 tablespoon fish sauce
- 1/2 tablespoon lime juice
- 1/2 teaspoon honey
- 1/2 clove garlic, minced
- 1/2 teaspoon grated ginger

Instructions:
1. Heat a pan over high heat. Sear the beef slices for 1-2 minutes on each side, or until desired doneness. Set aside.
2. In a large mixing bowl, combine bean sprouts, coriander leaves, mint leaves, and red onion.
3. Add pomelo segments and carrot to the salad mix.
4. In a small bowl, whisk together soy sauce, fish sauce, lime juice, honey, garlic, and ginger to make the dressing.
5. Pour the dressing over the salad and toss gently to combine.
6. Arrange the salad on a plate, top with seared beef slices, and sprinkle with crushed peanuts, sesame seeds, and red chili.
7. Garnish with a lime wedge and serve immediately.

Smoked Chicken and Endive Salad

Time: 20 mins

Ingredients:
- 4-6 ounces smoked chicken breast, thinly sliced
- 1 endive, leaves separated
- 1/4 cup radishes, thinly sliced
- 1/4 cup cucumber, thinly sliced
- 1 tablespoon fresh coriander leaves
- 1 tablespoon chopped peanuts
- Salt and pepper, to taste

Dressing:
- 2 tablespoons mayonnaise
- 1 teaspoon Dijon mustard
- 1 teaspoon honey
- 1 teaspoon apple cider vinegar
- Salt and pepper, to taste

Instructions:
1. Arrange endive leaves on a serving plate.
2. Layer sliced radishes, cucumber, and smoked chicken breast on top of the endive leaves.
3. In a small bowl, mix together mayonnaise, Dijon mustard, honey, and apple cider vinegar. Season with salt and pepper to taste.
4. Drizzle the dressing over the salad.
5. Garnish with fresh coriander leaves and chopped peanuts.
6. Season with additional salt and pepper to taste, if desired, and serve immediately.

Spicy Taco Salad with Beef and Chipotle Lime Dressing

Time: 25 mins

Ingredients:
- 3-4 ounces ground beef, cooked
- 1 cup chopped romaine lettuce
- 1/4 cup cooked and seasoned ground beef
- 1/4 cup shredded cheddar cheese
- 1/4 cup canned black beans, rinsed and drained
- 1/2 small tomato, diced
- 1/2 avocado, diced
- 1 tablespoon sliced red onions
- 1 tablespoon tortilla chips

Dressing:
- 1/2 teaspoon chipotle in adobo sauce, finely chopped
- 1/2 teaspoon lime juice
- 1 tablespoon olive oil
- 1/2 teaspoon honey
- Salt and pepper to taste

Instructions:
1. Place the chopped lettuce at the bottom of a large salad bowl.
2. Top the lettuce with cooked ground beef, shredded cheese, black beans, diced tomatoes, diced avocado, and sliced red onions.
3. In a small bowl, whisk together the chipotle in adobo sauce, lime juice, olive oil, honey, salt, and pepper until well combined.
4. Drizzle the dressing over the salad.
5. Garnish with tortilla chips.
6. Serve immediately and enjoy!

Sweet and Sour Chicken and Pineapple Salad

Time: 20 mins

Ingredients:
- 4-6 ounces cooked chicken breast, sliced
- 1/2 cup pineapple slices
- 1/4 cup cucumber, diced
- 1/2 cup red bell pepper, diced
- 1/4 red onion, thinly sliced
- Fresh cilantro leaves for garnish
- Fresh red chili, sliced for garnish
- 1 teaspoon sesame seeds

Dressing:
- 1 tablespoon sweet and sour sauce
- 1/2 tablespoon soy sauce
- 1/2 teaspoon rice vinegar
- 1/2 teaspoon honey
- 1/2 teaspoon sesame oil

Instructions:
1. Arrange the sliced cooked chicken breast in the center of a serving plate.
2. Place the pineapple slices around the chicken on the plate.
3. Scatter the diced cucumber and red bell pepper around the chicken and pineapple.
4. Add the thinly sliced red onion on top of the salad.
5. In a small bowl, whisk together the sweet and sour sauce, soy sauce, rice vinegar, honey, and sesame oil to create the dressing.
6. Drizzle the dressing over the salad.
7. Garnish with fresh cilantro leaves, sliced red chili, and sprinkle with sesame seeds.
8. Serve immediately and enjoy your sweet and sour delight.

Thinly Sliced Beef Salad with Miso Vinaigrette

Time: 25 mins

Ingredients:
- 3-4 ounces thinly sliced beef, preferably sirloin or ribeye
- 2 cups mixed salad greens
- 1/4 cup radishes, thinly sliced
- 1/4 cup cucumber, thinly sliced
- 1/4 cup sprouts
- 1 teaspoon sesame seeds

Dressing:
- 1 tablespoon miso paste
- 1 tablespoon rice vinegar
- 1 tablespoon soy sauce
- 1 teaspoon sesame oil
- 1 teaspoon honey
- 1/2 clove garlic, minced
- 1 teaspoon grated fresh ginger

Instructions:
1. Cook the beef to your preferred doneness, let it rest, then slice it thinly.
2. Arrange the mixed salad greens on a plate.
3. Distribute the sliced radishes, cucumber, and sprouts over the greens.
4. For the dressing, whisk together the miso paste, rice vinegar, soy sauce, sesame oil, honey, minced garlic, and grated ginger in a small bowl until smooth.
5. Arrange the beef slices on top of the salad.
6. Drizzle the miso vinaigrette over the beef and salad greens.
7. Sprinkle sesame seeds over the salad as a garnish.
8. Serve the salad immediately, offering a harmonious blend of flavors and textures.

Vegetarian Salads

Arugula and Soft Boiled Egg Salad

Time: 10 mins

Ingredients:
- 1 cup arugula leaves
- 1 soft boiled egg, halved
- 1/2 ripe avocado, sliced
- 6 cherry tomatoes, halved
- 1 tablespoon crumbled goat cheese
- 1 teaspoon hemp seeds (optional)
- Freshly ground black pepper, to taste

Dressing:
- 2 tablespoons olive oil
- 1 tablespoon balsamic vinegar
- 1/2 teaspoon Dijon mustard
- 1/2 teaspoon honey
- Salt, to taste

Instructions:
1. Prepare the soft boiled egg: bring water to a boil, gently place the egg in, and cook for 6-7 minutes for a runny yolk or 8-9 minutes for a firmer yolk. Once cooked, place in ice water to cool before peeling and halving.
2. In a small bowl, whisk together olive oil, balsamic vinegar, Dijon mustard, honey, and a pinch of salt to create the dressing.
3. Arrange the arugula leaves on a plate as the salad base.
4. Add the sliced avocado and cherry tomato halves on top of the arugula.
5. Place the soft boiled egg halves on the salad.
6. Sprinkle crumbled goat cheese and hemp seeds over the salad, if using.
7. Drizzle the dressing over the salad.
8. Finish with freshly ground black pepper to taste.
9. Serve immediately, enjoying the mix of warm egg and cool, crisp salad.

Arugula Salad with Fig, Pomegranate and Goat Cheese

Time: 10 mins

Ingredients:
- 1 cup arugula
- 4 fresh figs, quartered
- 1/4 cup pomegranate seeds
- 2 tablespoons walnuts, roughly chopped
- 1 ounce goat cheese, crumbled
- 1 tablespoon olive oil
- 1 teaspoon honey
- Salt to taste
- Black pepper to taste

Dressing:
- 2 tablespoons extra virgin olive oil
- 1 teaspoon balsamic vinegar
- 1/2 teaspoon honey
- A pinch of salt
- A pinch of freshly ground black pepper

Instructions:
1. Wash the arugula and pat dry with a paper towel. Place it in a serving bowl.
2. Add the quartered figs and pomegranate seeds to the bowl with the arugula.
3. Scatter the roughly chopped walnuts and crumbled goat cheese over the top.
4. In a small bowl, whisk together the olive oil, honey, salt, and black pepper until well combined. This will be used to lightly coat the leaves.
5. For the dressing, in another small bowl, combine extra virgin olive oil, balsamic vinegar, honey, salt, and black pepper. Whisk until the dressing emulsifies.
6. Drizzle the olive oil and honey mixture over the salad, then toss gently to coat the leaves and ingredients.
7. Drizzle the balsamic dressing over the salad just before serving.

Asparagus Salad with Feta and Pickled Onions

Time: 20 mins

Ingredients:
- 5 asparagus, trimmed and blanched
- 1/2 cup pickled red onions, thinly sliced
- 2 tablespoons feta cheese, crumbled
- 1 tablespoon parsley leaves, fresh

Dressing:
- 1 tablespoon extra virgin olive oil
- 1 teaspoon lemon juice
- 1/2 teaspoon honey
- Salt and freshly ground black pepper, to taste

Instructions:
1. Begin by blanching the asparagus: bring a pot of salted water to a boil, add asparagus and cook until just tender, about 3-4 minutes. Drain and plunge into an ice water bath to stop the cooking process.
2. For the dressing, in a small bowl, whisk together olive oil, lemon juice, honey, salt, and pepper until well combined.
3. Arrange the blanched asparagus on a serving platter.
4. Scatter the pickled red onions and crumbled feta cheese over the asparagus.
5. Drizzle the dressing over the salad, ensuring even coverage.
6. Garnish with parsley leaves.
7. Serve immediately, or chill in the refrigerator for 10 minutes to allow flavors to meld.

Avocado Caprese Tower Salad

Time: 10 mins

Ingredients:
- 1/2 ripe avocado, sliced
- 1 large ripe tomato, sliced
- 2-3 small fresh mozzarella cheese balls (approximately 3 oz)
- Fresh basil leaves
- Pine nuts for garnish (optional)

Dressing:
- 1 tablespoon balsamic glaze
- 1/2 tablespoon extra virgin olive oil
- Salt and freshly ground black pepper, to taste

Instructions:
1. On a serving plate, start by layering slices of tomato, followed by slices of avocado.
2. Place the fresh mozzarella balls on top of the avocado.
3. Garnish with fresh basil leaves and sprinkle pine nuts over the salad if desired.
4. Drizzle balsamic glaze and olive oil over the tower.
5. Season with salt and freshly ground black pepper to taste.
6. Serve immediately as a fresh appetizer or a light, refreshing meal.

Bocconcini and Arugula Salad with Balsamic Glaze

Time: 10 mins

Ingredients:
- 1 cup arugula leaves, fresh
- 4 cherry tomatoes, halved
- 3 bocconcini cheese balls, halved (approximately 3-4 oz)
- 1 tablespoon balsamic glaze
- A pinch of sea salt
- A pinch of freshly ground black pepper

Dressing:
- 1 teaspoon extra virgin olive oil
- 1 teaspoon balsamic vinegar
- Salt and pepper to taste

Instructions:
1. Wash the arugula leaves and pat them dry. Arrange them as a bed on a serving plate.
2. Place the halved cherry tomatoes and bocconcini cheese on top of the arugula leaves, distributing them evenly.
3. In a small bowl, whisk together the extra virgin olive oil, balsamic vinegar, salt, and pepper to make the dressing.
4. Drizzle the dressing over the salad.
5. Drizzle the balsamic glaze in a zigzag pattern over the salad for a decorative and flavorful finish.
6. Sprinkle a pinch of sea salt and freshly ground black pepper over the salad to taste.
7. Serve immediately as a fresh appetizer or a light meal.

Brussels Sprout Slaw with Hazelnut and Pomegranate

Time: 15 mins

Ingredients:
- 1 cup shredded Brussels sprouts
- 2 tablespoons pomegranate seeds
- 2 tablespoons chopped hazelnuts
- 1/2 small red onion, thinly sliced
- Fresh parsley, chopped (for garnish)

Dressing:
- 1 tablespoon olive oil
- 1 tablespoon apple cider vinegar
- 1 teaspoon honey
- Salt and pepper to taste

Instructions:
1. Trim the ends of the Brussels sprouts and remove any damaged outer leaves. Use a food processor or a sharp knife to shred the Brussels sprouts finely.
2. In a mixing bowl, combine the shredded Brussels sprouts with the thinly sliced red onion, pomegranate seeds, and chopped hazelnuts.
3. In a small bowl, whisk together the olive oil, apple cider vinegar, honey, salt, and pepper to create the dressing.
4. Pour the dressing over the slaw mixture and toss well to coat all the ingredients evenly.
5. Let the slaw sit for about 5 minutes to allow the flavors to meld.
6. Garnish with chopped fresh parsley before serving.
7. Enjoy this colorful and crunchy slaw as a refreshing side dish or a healthy main course.

Burrata with Heirloom Tomatoes and Basil

Time: 10 mins

Ingredients:
- 2 small burrata cheese (approximately 3-4 oz)
- 1 cup heirloom tomatoes, mixed colors, sliced
- Fresh basil leaves for garnish
- 2 small slices of ciabatta bread, grilled
- Extra virgin olive oil for drizzling
- Balsamic reduction for drizzling
- Sea salt to taste
- Freshly ground black pepper to taste

Dressing:
- 1 tablespoon extra virgin olive oil
- 1/2 tablespoon balsamic reduction
- Salt and pepper to taste

Instructions:
1. Place the sliced heirloom tomatoes on a plate, arranging them around the edge.
2. Carefully place the burrata cheese in the center of the plate.
3. Scatter fresh basil leaves over the tomatoes and burrata.
4. In a small bowl, whisk together the extra virgin olive oil, balsamic reduction, salt, and pepper to create the dressing.
5. Drizzle the dressing over the burrata and tomatoes.
6. Drizzle additional balsamic reduction over the salad for a more intense flavor and decorative appeal.
7. Season the salad with sea salt and freshly ground black pepper.
8. Serve the grilled ciabatta bread on the side.
9. Enjoy this dish immediately, while the bread is warm and the burrata is creamy and fresh.

Butternut Squash Burrito Bowl

Time: 55 mins

Ingredients:
- 1/2 cup cooked brown rice
- 1/2 cup black beans, rinsed and drained
- 1/2 cup corn kernels, fresh or thawed if frozen
- 1/2 cup butternut squash, cubed and roasted
- 1/2 cup cherry tomatoes, halved
- 1/2 avocado, sliced
- Fresh cilantro leaves for garnish
- Lime wedges for serving

Dressing:
- 2 tablespoons Greek yogurt
- 1 tablespoon fresh lime juice
- 1/2 teaspoon garlic powder
- 1/2 teaspoon onion powder
- Salt and pepper to taste

Instructions:
1. Begin by cooking the brown rice according to package instructions and set aside to cool.
2. Preheat the oven to 400°F (200°C). Toss the cubed butternut squash with olive oil, salt, and pepper, and spread it out on a baking sheet. Roast for 25-30 minutes or until tender and slightly caramelized.
3. In a serving bowl, start by laying down a base of cooked brown rice.
4. Arrange the black beans, corn kernels, roasted butternut squash, and cherry tomato halves on top of the rice.
5. In a small bowl, mix together the Greek yogurt, lime juice, garlic powder, onion powder, salt, and pepper to make the dressing.
6. Drizzle the dressing generously over the burrito bowl.
7. Garnish with avocado slices and fresh cilantro leaves.
8. Serve with lime wedges on the side for an extra zing.

Creamy Cucumber and Radish Salad

Time: 10 mins

Ingredients:
- 1/2 large cucumber, thinly sliced
- 4 radishes, thinly sliced
- 1 tablespoon fresh dill, chopped
- Salt and freshly ground black pepper to taste

Dressing:
- 3 tablespoons Greek yogurt
- 1 tablespoon mayonnaise (optional, for extra creaminess)
- 1 teaspoon apple cider vinegar
- 1/2 teaspoon honey
- A pinch of garlic powder

Instructions:
1. In a serving bowl, combine the thinly sliced cucumber and radishes.
2. In a separate small bowl, mix together the Greek yogurt, mayonnaise (if using), apple cider vinegar, honey, and garlic powder to make the dressing.
3. Pour the dressing over the sliced vegetables and toss gently to coat.
4. Season the salad with salt and pepper to taste.
5. Garnish with fresh dill.
6. Serve immediately or chill in the refrigerator for 30 minutes before serving to allow the flavors to meld.

Crunchy Apple Walnut Salad

Time: 10 mins

Ingredients:
- 1 cup chopped romaine lettuce
- 1/2 medium apple, cored and sliced
- 1 tablespoon walnuts, roughly chopped
- 1 tablespoon raisins
- 1 ounce blue cheese, crumbled (optional)

Dressing:
- 2 tablespoons Greek yogurt
- 1 tablespoon mayonnaise
- 1/2 teaspoon honey
- 1/2 teaspoon lemon juice
- A pinch of salt
- A pinch of black pepper
- Fresh dill, finely chopped (to taste)

Instructions:
1. Begin by preparing the dressing: in a small bowl, whisk together Greek yogurt, mayonnaise, honey, lemon juice, salt, pepper, and chopped dill until well combined. Adjust the seasoning to your taste.
2. In a serving bowl, place the chopped romaine lettuce as the base.
3. Add the sliced apples on top of the lettuce, distributing them evenly.
4. Sprinkle the chopped walnuts and raisins over the apples.
5. If using, crumble blue cheese and distribute it over the salad.
6. Drizzle the prepared dressing over the salad just before serving.
7. Gently toss the salad to ensure all the ingredients are evenly coated with the dressing.

Edamame Salad with Sesame Cashew Lime Dressing

Time: 20 mins

Ingredients:
- 1 cup shredded purple cabbage
- 1/2 cup shelled edamame, cooked and cooled
- 1 medium carrot, julienned
- 1/2 bell pepper, thinly sliced
- 1 green onion, sliced
- Fresh cilantro leaves for garnish
- Sesame seeds for garnish
- 1 tablespoon peanuts, roughly chopped

Dressing:
- 2 tablespoons cashew butter
- Juice of 1/2 lime
- 1 tablespoon soy sauce
- 1 tablespoon sesame oil
- 1/2 teaspoon honey
- 1/2 clove garlic, minced
- 1/2 teaspoon grated ginger

Instructions:
1. In a large bowl, combine the shredded cabbage, cooked edamame, julienned carrot, sliced bell pepper, and green onion.
2. In a small bowl, whisk together the cashew butter, lime juice, soy sauce, sesame oil, honey, minced garlic, and grated ginger until smooth to create the dressing.
3. Pour the dressing over the salad and toss to coat all the ingredients evenly.
4. Garnish with fresh cilantro leaves, peanuts and a sprinkle of sesame seeds.
5. Serve immediately or let it sit for about 10 minutes to allow the flavors to infuse before serving.

Freekeh Salad with Pomegranate and Goat Cheese

Time: 40 mins

Ingredients:
- 1 cup cooked freekeh
- 1/4 cup pomegranate seeds
- 1 tablespoon goat cheese, crumbled
- 1 tablespoon pine nuts, toasted
- 1 tablespoon fresh mint leaves
- Salt to taste
- Black pepper to taste

Dressing:
- 2 tablespoons olive oil
- 1 tablespoon lemon juice
- 1/2 teaspoon honey
- 1/2 teaspoon ground cumin
- Salt and pepper to taste

Instructions:
1. Cook the freekeh according to the package instructions until it is tender and then let it cool.
2. In a large bowl, mix the cooled freekeh with pomegranate seeds, crumbled goat cheese, and toasted pine nuts.
3. Add the roughly torn mint leaves to the salad and toss gently.
4. For the dressing, whisk together olive oil, lemon juice, honey, ground cumin, salt, and pepper in a small bowl until well combined.
5. Drizzle the dressing over the salad and toss until everything is evenly coated.
6. Season with additional salt and pepper if needed.
7. Serve the salad at room temperature or chilled, as preferred.

Gado-Gado with Peanut Sauce

Time: 30 mins

Ingredients:
- 1 cup green beans, trimmed and cut into 2-inch pieces
- 1 medium potato, sliced and boiled
- 1 hard-boiled egg, peeled and halved
- 1 cup of mixed salad greens
- 1/2 cup fried shallots (for garnish)
- Salt to taste

Peanut Sauce:
- 1/2 cup natural peanut butter
- 1 tablespoon soy sauce
- 1 tablespoon lime juice
- 1 teaspoon brown sugar
- 1/2 teaspoon garlic, finely grated
- 1/2 teaspoon ginger, finely grated
- 1/2 cup water (or as needed for desired consistency)
- Chili flakes to taste (optional)

Instructions:
1. Bring a pot of water to a boil, add a pinch of salt, and blanch the green beans for about 3 minutes until tender-crisp. Drain and rinse with cold water to stop the cooking process.
2. Arrange the mixed salad greens on a serving plate.
3. Place the blanched green beans, boiled potato slices, and halved hard-boiled egg on top of the greens.
4. To make the peanut sauce, whisk together the peanut butter, soy sauce, lime juice, brown sugar, garlic, ginger, and water in a bowl. Adjust the consistency with water as needed. Add chili flakes if desired for some heat.
5. Drizzle a generous amount of the peanut sauce over the arranged ingredients.
6. Garnish with fried shallots.
7. Serve immediately, with extra peanut sauce on the side if desired.

Greek Chickpea Salad with Corn and Greek Yogurt

Time: 15 mins

Ingredients:
- 1/2 cup chickpeas, drained and rinsed
- 1/4 cup cherry tomatoes, halved
- 1/4 cup cucumber, diced
- 2 tablespoons red onion, thinly sliced
- 2 tablespoons yellow bell pepper, diced
- 1 tablespoon corn kernels, cooked
- 1 tablespoon feta cheese, crumbled
- 1 tablespoon Greek yogurt
- Fresh parsley, chopped (for garnish)

Dressing:
- 1 tablespoon olive oil
- 1/2 tablespoon lemon juice
- 1/2 teaspoon red wine vinegar
- 1/4 teaspoon dried oregano
- Salt and pepper, to taste
- Optional: A small clove of garlic, minced

Instructions:
1. Prepare the Ingredients: Combine the chickpeas, cherry tomatoes, cucumber, red onion, yellow bell pepper, and corn kernels in a mixing bowl.
2. Mix the Dressing: Whisk together the olive oil, lemon juice, red wine vinegar, dried oregano, minced garlic (if using), and a pinch of salt and pepper in a small bowl.
3. Combine the Salad: Toss the salad with the dressing to coat all the ingredients well.
4. Assemble the Dish: Transfer to a serving plate and dollop the Greek yogurt on top. Sprinkle with crumbled feta cheese.
5. Garnish: Garnish with fresh parsley and serve immediately.

Greek Salad

Time: 10 mins

Ingredients:
- 1 cup cucumber, sliced
- 1 cup cherry tomatoes, halved
- 1/2 cup red onion, thinly sliced
- 1/2 cup Kalamata olives
- 1/2 cup feta cheese, crumbled
- 1 tablespoon fresh parsley, chopped
- Salt and pepper to taste

Dressing:
- 2 tablespoons extra virgin olive oil
- 1 tablespoon red wine vinegar
- 1 teaspoon dried oregano
- Salt and pepper to taste

Instructions:
1. In a large bowl, combine sliced cucumber, halved cherry tomatoes, thinly sliced red onion, and Kalamata olives.
2. Crumble feta cheese over the top of the salad.
3. Sprinkle chopped parsley for a fresh herbaceous note.
4. In a small bowl, whisk together extra virgin olive oil, red wine vinegar, dried oregano, salt, and pepper to create the dressing.
5. Drizzle the dressing over the salad and toss gently to combine.
6. Season with additional salt and pepper if needed.
7. Serve immediately or chill in the refrigerator for about 15 minutes before serving to let the flavors meld.

Grilled Halloumi and Citrus Salad

Time: 15 mins

Ingredients:
- 2 slices of halloumi cheese, about 1/4 inch thick (approximately 2-3 oz)
- 1 medium carrot, peeled and thinly sliced
- 1 small orange, peeled and segmented
- 1/2 cup fresh arugula
- 1/2 tablespoon chopped fresh parsley
- 1/2 tablespoon pine nuts, toasted

Dressing:
- 1 tablespoon extra-virgin olive oil
- 1 teaspoon balsamic vinegar
- Salt and pepper to taste

Instructions:
1. Heat a non-stick grill pan over medium heat.
2. Add the halloumi slices and grill for about 2 minutes on each side, or until they have nice grill marks.
3. Arrange the arugula on a plate and layer the carrot slices and orange segments on top.
4. Place the grilled halloumi on the salad.
5. Sprinkle with parsley and toasted pine nuts.
6. Whisk together the olive oil, balsamic vinegar, salt, and pepper, and drizzle over the salad.

Grilled Peach, Arugula, and Goat Cheese Stack

Time: 15 mins

Ingredients:
- 1 ripe peach, cut into rounds
- 1 tablespoon olive oil
- 1/2 cup arugula (rocket) leaves
- 2 tablespoons goat cheese, crumbled

Dressing:
- 1 tablespoon balsamic glaze
- Salt and pepper to taste
- A sprinkle of toasted pumpkin seeds (optional)

Instructions:
1. Preheat your grill to medium-high heat.
2. Brush the peach rounds with olive oil and season with a pinch of salt.
3. Grill the peach rounds for about 2-3 minutes on each side, or until grill marks appear and the peaches are slightly softened.
4. On a serving plate, create a base layer with a few arugula leaves.
5. Stack a grilled peach round on top, then add a sprinkle of crumbled goat cheese.
6. Repeat the layers until all the peach rounds are used.
7. Garnish the stack with more arugula leaves on top and around the base.
8. Drizzle with balsamic glaze and sprinkle with toasted pumpkin seeds if desired.
9. Season with salt and pepper to taste.
10. Serve immediately as an elegant starter or a light meal.

Grilled Zucchini Salad with Parmesan and Pine Nuts

Time: 15 mins

Ingredients:
- 1 medium zucchini, thinly sliced lengthwise
- 1/2 cup arugula
- 2 tablespoons pine nuts, toasted
- 2 tablespoons shavings of Parmesan cheese
- Salt and freshly ground black pepper to taste

Dressing:
- 2 tablespoons extra virgin olive oil
- 1 tablespoon fresh lemon juice
- 1 teaspoon honey
- A pinch of salt and pepper

Instructions:
1. Preheat a grill or grill pan over medium heat.
2. Lightly oil the zucchini slices and season them with salt and pepper.
3. Grill the zucchini slices for about 1-2 minutes on each side until tender and grill marks appear.
4. In a bowl, whisk together the olive oil, lemon juice, honey, and a pinch of salt and pepper to make the dressing.
5. Arrange the arugula on a plate and top with the grilled zucchini slices.
6. Drizzle the dressing over the salad.
7. Sprinkle toasted pine nuts and Parmesan shavings over the top.
8. Season with additional salt and pepper if desired.

Herbed Potato Salad

Time: 35 mins

Ingredients:
- 1 cup baby potatoes, halved
- 1 tablespoon green onions, chopped
- 1/2 tablespoon fresh dill, chopped
- 1/2 tablespoon fresh parsley, chopped
- Salt and pepper to taste

Dressing:
- 1 tablespoon Greek yogurt
- 1 teaspoon Dijon mustard
- 1 teaspoon honey
- 1 teaspoon apple cider vinegar
- Salt and pepper to taste

Instructions:
1. Place the potatoes in a pot and cover with cold water. Bring to a boil and cook until the potatoes are tender, about 15-20 minutes.
2. Drain the potatoes and let them cool for a few minutes.
3. In a large bowl, combine the green onions, dill, parsley, salt, and pepper.
4. Add the cooled potatoes to the herb mixture.
5. In a small bowl, whisk together Greek yogurt, Dijon mustard, honey, apple cider vinegar, salt, and pepper.
6. Pour the dressing over the potatoes and herbs and gently mix until the potatoes are well coated.
7. Refrigerate the salad for at least 1 hour before serving to allow the flavors to meld.

Honey Roasted Fig and Goat Cheese Salad

Time: 25 mins

Ingredients:
- 4 small fresh figs, halved
- 1 cup fresh spinach leaves
- 1 tablespoon crumbled goat cheese
- 1 tablespoon walnuts, roughly chopped

Dressing:
- 1 tablespoon honey
- 1 tablespoon extra-virgin olive oil
- 1 teaspoon balsamic vinegar
- Salt and pepper to taste

Instructions:
1. Preheat your oven to 375°F (190°C).
2. Place the fig halves on a baking sheet, cut side up.
3. Drizzle 1 tablespoon of honey over the figs and roast in the oven for 15 minutes, until they are soft and slightly caramelized.
4. While the figs are roasting, arrange the spinach leaves on a serving plate.
5. Once the figs are done, allow them to cool for a few minutes, then place them on top of the spinach.
6. Sprinkle the crumbled goat cheese and walnuts over the salad.
7. In a small bowl, whisk together the remaining honey, olive oil, balsamic vinegar, salt, and pepper to create the dressing.
8. Drizzle the dressing over the salad just before serving.

Kale and Roasted Cauliflower Salad

Time: 35 mins

Ingredients:
- 1 cup kale, chopped
- 1/2 cup cauliflower florets
- 1 soft boiled egg, halved
- 1 tablespoon almonds, toasted
- 1 tablespoon chickpeas, roasted
- Salt and pepper to taste

Dressing:
- 1 tablespoon tahini
- 1 tablespoon Greek yogurt
- 1/2 tablespoon lemon juice
- 1/2 teaspoon honey
- 1/2 garlic clove, minced
- Water to thin (as needed)
- Salt and pepper to taste

Instructions:
1. Preheat the oven to 400°F (200°C).
2. Spread the cauliflower florets on a baking sheet, drizzle with olive oil, and season with salt and pepper. Roast for 20 minutes or until tender and slightly caramelized.
3. Wash the kale and pat dry. Remove the stems and chop the leaves.
4. Arrange the kale on a plate. Add the roasted cauliflower and chickpeas.
5. Place the toasted almonds and the halved boiled egg on top of the salad.
6. In a small bowl, whisk together tahini, Greek yogurt, lemon juice, honey, minced garlic, and enough water to reach a pourable consistency. Season with salt and pepper.
7. Drizzle the dressing over the salad just before serving.

Kale and Spinach Falafel Salad

Time: 15 mins

Ingredients:
- 1 cup fresh kale, chopped
- 1 cup fresh spinach, chopped
- 3-4 falafel balls
- 1/2 ripe avocado, sliced
- 1/2 cup cherry tomatoes, halved (assorted colors)
- 1 tablespoon sliced red onion
- 1 tablespoon chopped fresh parsley (for garnish)
- Salt and pepper to taste

Dressing:
- 1 tablespoon Greek yogurt
- 1 teaspoon lemon juice
- 1/2 teaspoon dried dill
- 1/2 clove garlic, minced
- Salt and pepper to taste

Instructions:
1. Wash and dry the kale and spinach leaves. Chop them roughly and place them in a serving bowl as the salad base.
2. Heat the falafel balls as per the package instructions if not freshly made. Arrange them on top of the greens.
3. Slice the avocado and red onion. Halve the cherry tomatoes. Distribute these evenly over the greens.
4. For the dressing, combine the Greek yogurt, lemon juice, dried dill, minced garlic, salt, and pepper in a small bowl. Stir until well mixed.
5. Drizzle the dressing over the salad. Garnish with chopped parsley.
6. Season with a pinch of salt and pepper to your taste. Serve immediately.

Kale, Tomato, and Pickled Rhubarb Salad

Time: 15 mins

Ingredients:
- 1 cup kale, stems removed and leaves torn
- 1/2 cup cherry tomatoes, halved
- 1/2 cup pickled rhubarb, sliced
- 1 tablespoon red onion, thinly sliced
- 1 tablespoon pine nuts (optional)

Dressing:
- 1 tablespoon olive oil
- 1/2 tablespoon apple cider vinegar
- 1 teaspoon Dijon mustard
- 1/2 teaspoon honey
- Salt and pepper to taste

Instructions:
1. If you're pickling your own rhubarb, do this ahead of time by slicing and soaking the rhubarb in a mixture of vinegar, sugar, and water.
2. In a large bowl, combine the torn kale, halved cherry tomatoes, and pickled rhubarb.
3. In a small bowl, whisk together the olive oil, apple cider vinegar, Dijon mustard, honey, salt, and pepper until emulsified.
4. Pour the dressing over the salad and toss to coat the ingredients thoroughly.
5. Top the salad with thinly sliced red onion and pine nuts if using.
6. Serve immediately, or let it sit for a few minutes to allow the flavors to meld.

Mint and Tomato Mediterranean Pearly Couscous Salad

Time: 15 mins

Ingredients:
- 1/2 cup cooked pearly couscous
- 1/2 cup cherry tomatoes, halved
- 1/2 cup diced cucumber
- 1/2 tablespoon pine nuts
- 1 tablespoon chopped fresh mint
- Salt and black pepper to taste

Dressing:
- 1 tablespoon extra virgin olive oil
- 1/2 tablespoon lemon juice
- 1/2 teaspoon honey
- 1/2 teaspoon dried oregano
- Salt and pepper to taste

Instructions:
1. Prepare the couscous according to the package instructions and let it cool.
2. In a salad bowl, combine the cooked couscous, cherry tomatoes, cucumber, and pine nuts.
3. In a small bowl, whisk together the olive oil, lemon juice, honey, oregano, salt, and pepper to create the dressing.
4. Pour the dressing over the couscous mixture and toss to combine.
5. Gently fold in the chopped mint.
6. Adjust the seasoning with salt and pepper to your taste.
7. Serve chilled or at room temperature. Garnish with extra mint leaves if desired.

Pear Salad with Roquefort and Walnuts

Time: 10 mins

Ingredients:
- 1 ripe pear, thinly sliced
- 1 cup arugula
- 1/2 cup Roquefort cheese, crumbled
- 1 tablespoon chopped walnuts
- Fresh herbs for garnish (optional)

Dressing:
- 1 tablespoon extra virgin olive oil
- 1/2 tablespoon white balsamic vinegar
- 1/2 teaspoon Dijon mustard
- 1/2 teaspoon honey
- Salt and freshly ground black pepper to taste

Instructions:
1. Arrange the arugula on a serving plate.
2. Layer the thinly sliced pear over the arugula.
3. Sprinkle the crumbled Roquefort cheese and chopped walnuts over the pears.
4. In a small bowl, whisk together the olive oil, white balsamic vinegar, Dijon mustard, honey, salt, and black pepper to create the dressing.
5. Drizzle the dressing over the salad just before serving.
6. Garnish with fresh herbs if desired.
7. Serve immediately as a fresh starter or side to your main dish.

Plums and Basil Salad with Balsamic Glaze

Time: 10 mins

Ingredients:
- 4 ripe plums, pitted and sliced
- A handful of fresh basil leaves
- 1 tablespoon Parmesan cheese, shaved
- 1 tablespoon chopped walnuts
- Salt, to taste
- Freshly ground black pepper, to taste

Dressing:
- 2 tablespoons balsamic glaze

Instructions:
1. Arrange the plum slices on a plate, alternating with basil leaves.
2. Sprinkle the shaved Parmesan cheese over the plums.
3. Add the chopped walnuts evenly across the salad.
4. Season with salt and freshly ground black pepper to taste.
5. Drizzle the balsamic glaze over the salad just before serving.

Pomegranate and Fennel Salad

Time: 15 mins

Ingredients:
- 1/2 cup pomegranate seeds
- 1 small fennel bulb, thinly sliced
- 1/4 cup pumpkin seeds
- 1 tablespoon fresh dill, chopped

Dressing:
- 3 tablespoons olive oil
- 1 tablespoon lemon juice
- 1 teaspoon honey
- Salt and pepper to taste

Instructions:
1. In a large bowl, combine the pomegranate seeds, sliced fennel, and pumpkin seeds.
2. In a small bowl, whisk together the olive oil, lemon juice, honey, salt, and pepper to create the dressing.
3. Pour the dressing over the salad ingredients and toss gently to combine.
4. Garnish with the chopped dill.
5. Serve immediately or refrigerate until ready to serve.

Quinoa and Pomegranate Salad with Orange

Time: 35 mins

Ingredients:
- 1/4 cup cooked quinoa
- 1/4 cup kale or leafy greens, chopped
- 2 tablespoons fresh parsley, finely chopped
- 2 tablespoons pomegranate seeds
- 1 tablespoon sliced almonds
- 1 orange, peeled and segmented
- 1/2 garlic clove, thinly sliced

Dressing:
- 1/2 tablespoon orange juice (freshly squeezed from the orange)
- 1/2 tablespoon extra virgin olive oil
- 1/2 teaspoon honey or maple syrup
- Salt and pepper to taste

Instructions:
1. In a large bowl, combine the cooked quinoa, chopped kale or leafy greens, and finely chopped parsley.
2. Add the pomegranate seeds and orange segments to the bowl.
3. In a dry pan, lightly toast the sliced almonds over medium heat until golden brown, then add to the salad.
4. For the dressing, whisk together the orange juice, olive oil, honey or maple syrup, salt, and pepper in a small bowl.
5. Drizzle the dressing over the salad and toss to combine.
6. Top the salad with thinly sliced garlic.
7. Serve immediately or chill in the refrigerator before serving.

Rainbow Buddha Bowl

Time: 20 mins

Ingredients:
- 1/4 cup romaine lettuce, chopped
- 1/2 cup red cabbage, shredded
- 1/2 avocado, sliced
- 1/4 cup chickpeas, roasted
- 1/4 cup mango, cubed
- 1/4 cup pineapple, cubed
- 1 tablespoon raw pumpkin seeds
- 1 tablespoon hemp seeds
- 1/2 tablespoon sesame seeds
- 1/2 tablespoon olive oil
- Salt and pepper to taste

Dressing:
- 1 tablespoon extra virgin olive oil
- 1/2 tablespoon apple cider vinegar
- 1/2 teaspoon honey
- 1/2 teaspoon mustard
- Salt and pepper to taste

Instructions:
1. Arrange the chopped romaine lettuce as a bed in a large bowl.
2. Neatly organize the shredded red cabbage, sliced avocado, roasted chickpeas, cubed mango, and cubed pineapple on top of the lettuce in separate sections.
3. Sprinkle raw pumpkin seeds, hemp seeds, and sesame seeds over the arranged ingredients.
4. In a small bowl, whisk together extra virgin olive oil, apple cider vinegar, honey, mustard, salt, and pepper to create the dressing.
5. Drizzle the dressing over the Buddha bowl before serving.
6. Finish with a drizzle of olive oil and a sprinkle of salt and pepper to enhance the flavors.

Red Cabbage Coleslaw

Time: 15 mins

Ingredients:
- 1/2 cup shredded red cabbage
- 1/4 cup shredded carrots
- Fresh parsley for garnish

Dressing:
- 2 tablespoons mayonnaise
- 1/2 teaspoon apple cider vinegar
- 1/2 teaspoon Dijon mustard
- 1/2 teaspoon sugar
- Salt and pepper to taste

Instructions:
1. Arrange the chopped romaine lettuce as a bed in a large bowl.
2. In a large bowl, combine the shredded red cabbage and carrots.
3. In a small bowl, mix together the mayonnaise, apple cider vinegar, Dijon mustard, sugar, salt, and pepper to create the dressing.
4. Pour the dressing over the cabbage and carrots and toss to coat thoroughly.
5. Garnish with fresh parsley.
6. Refrigerate for at least 30 minutes before serving to allow the flavors to meld.
7. Serve chilled as a side dish to your favorite meals.

Roasted Beetroot and Feta Salad

Time: 1 hour and 15 mins

Ingredients:
- 1 medium beetroot, roasted and sliced
- 2 tablespoons feta cheese, crumbled
- 1/2 teaspoon fresh dill, finely chopped
- 1 teaspoon olive oil
- 1/2 teaspoon balsamic vinegar
- Salt and pepper to taste
- Optional: a sprinkle of sesame seeds

Dressing:
- 1 teaspoon olive oil
- 1 teaspoon balsamic vinegar
- A pinch of salt
- A pinch of freshly ground black pepper

Instructions:
1. Preheat your oven to 375°F (190°C). Wrap the beetroots in foil and place them on a baking tray. Roast in the oven for about 1 hour or until tender when pierced with a fork.
2. Once roasted, allow the beetroots to cool, then peel and slice them into thick rounds.
3. Arrange the beetroot slices on a plate.
4. Crumble feta cheese over the beetroot slices.
5. Sprinkle the finely chopped fresh dill across the salad.
6. In a small bowl, whisk together olive oil, balsamic vinegar, salt, and pepper to create the dressing.
7. Drizzle the dressing over the salad.
8. Optionally, sprinkle a small amount of sesame seeds over the salad for added texture and flavor.

Roasted Sweet Potatoes and Chickpeas Salad

Time: 45 mins

Ingredients:
- 1 medium sweet potato, thinly sliced
- 1/2 cup canned chickpeas, rinsed and drained
- 1/4 small red onion, thinly sliced
- 1 cup mixed salad greens
- 1 ounce feta cheese, crumbled
- 1 tbsp olive oil
- Salt to taste
- Black pepper to taste

Dressing:
- 2 tbsp olive oil
- 1 tbsp balsamic vinegar
- 1/2 tsp honey
- 1/4 tsp mustard
- Salt and pepper to taste

Instructions:
1. Preheat your oven to 400°F (200°C).
2. Arrange the sweet potato slices on a baking sheet in a single layer. Drizzle with olive oil and season with salt and pepper. Roast in the oven for 25-30 minutes or until tender and slightly caramelized.
3. While the sweet potatoes are roasting, prepare the dressing by whisking together olive oil, balsamic vinegar, honey, mustard, salt, and pepper in a small bowl until emulsified.
4. In a salad bowl, combine the mixed salad greens, roasted sweet potatoes, chickpeas, and red onion.
5. Drizzle the dressing over the salad and toss gently to coat.
6. Top the salad with crumbled feta cheese and serve immediately.

Roasted Vegetables Couscous

Time: 40 mins

Ingredients:
- 1/4 cup couscous, cooked according to package instructions
- 1/2 zucchini, chopped
- 1/2 red bell pepper, chopped
- 1/2 yellow bell pepper, chopped
- 1/2 red onion, chopped
- 1/2 eggplant, chopped
- Olive oil for roasting
- Fresh parsley, chopped for garnish

Dressing:
- 3 tablespoons olive oil
- 1 tablespoon lemon juice
- 1/2 garlic clove, minced
- 1/2 teaspoon ground cumin
- 1/2 teaspoon paprika
- Salt and pepper to taste

Instructions:
1. Preheat the oven to 425°F (220°C).
2. Toss the zucchini, red bell pepper, yellow bell pepper, red onion, and eggplant with olive oil and season with salt and pepper.
3. Spread the vegetables on a baking sheet in a single layer.
4. Roast for about 25 minutes, until the vegetables are tender and caramelized.
5. Prepare the couscous according to the package instructions.
6. Whisk together the olive oil, lemon juice, minced garlic, cumin, paprika, salt, and pepper to create the dressing.
7. Fluff the couscous with a fork and place it in a serving dish.
8. Top the couscous with the roasted vegetables.
9. Drizzle the dressing over the vegetables and couscous.
10. Garnish with chopped fresh parsley before serving.

Sauteed Vegetable and Noodle Salad

Time: 25 mins

Ingredients:
- 1 cup cooked rice noodles, cooled
- 1/2 red bell pepper, thinly sliced
- 1/2 yellow bell pepper, thinly sliced
- 1/2 zucchini, julienned
- 1 carrot, julienned
- 1 tablespoon fresh cilantro leaves
- 1/2 teaspoon sesame seeds

Dressing:
- 1/2 tablespoon soy sauce
- 1/2 teaspoon lime juice
- 1/2 tablespoon honey
- 1/2 teaspoon chili flakes (adjust to taste)
- 1/2 garlic clove, minced
- 1/2 teaspoon grated fresh ginger
- 1/2 teaspoon sesame oil

Instructions:
1. Heat a pan over medium heat and sauté the bell peppers, zucchini, and carrot until just tender, about 5 minutes.
2. In a large bowl, combine the sautéed vegetables with the cooked rice noodles.
3. In a small bowl, whisk together the soy sauce, lime juice, honey, chili flakes, minced garlic, grated ginger, and sesame oil to create the chili-lime dressing.
4. Pour the dressing over the noodle and vegetable mixture and toss to combine.
5. Garnish with fresh cilantro leaves and sesame seeds.
6. Serve the salad warm or at room temperature.

Shaved Fennel Salad with Orange and Almonds

Time: 20 mins

Ingredients:
- 1 large fennel bulb, thinly shaved
- 2 oranges, peeled and segments cut out
- 2 tablespoons slivered almonds, toasted
- 1/4 cup fresh parsley leaves
- 1/4 cup fresh dill
- 1 tablespoon olive oil
- Salt and pepper, to taste

Dressing:
- 3 tablespoons orange juice
- 1 tablespoon white wine vinegar
- 1 tablespoon olive oil
- 1 teaspoon honey
- Salt and pepper, to taste

Instructions:
1. Use a mandoline or sharp knife to shave the fennel bulb into thin slices.
2. In a bowl, combine shaved fennel, orange segments, parsley, and dill.
3. In a separate small bowl, whisk together the dressing ingredients: orange juice, white wine vinegar, olive oil, honey, salt, and pepper.
4. Drizzle the dressing over the fennel and orange mixture and toss gently to combine.
5. Transfer the salad to a serving plate and sprinkle toasted almonds over the top.
6. Season with additional salt and pepper to taste and serve immediately.

Spicy Greens Salad with Pomegranate Gremolata

Time: 15 mins

Ingredients:
- 1 cup mixed spicy greens (arugula, mustard greens, etc.)
- 1/4 cup pomegranate seeds
- 1/4 cup shredded carrots
- 1/2 apple, thinly sliced
- 1/4 cup pine nuts, toasted
- Salt and pepper, to taste

Dressing:
- 1 tablespoon olive oil
- 1/2 teaspoon balsamic vinegar
- 1/2 teaspoon honey
- 1/2 small garlic clove, minced
- Salt and pepper, to taste

Instructions:
1. In a large salad bowl, combine the mixed greens, pomegranate seeds, shredded carrots, and sliced apple.
2. In a dry pan, lightly toast the pine nuts over medium heat until golden, then let them cool.
3. Add the toasted pine nuts and crumbled feta cheese to the salad bowl.
4. In a small bowl, whisk together olive oil, balsamic vinegar, honey, and minced garlic to create the dressing. Season with salt and pepper to taste.
5. Drizzle the dressing over the salad and toss gently to combine all the ingredients.
6. Serve the salad immediately, optionally with dressing on the side.

Spinach, Strawberry, and Feta Salad

Time: 10 mins

Ingredients:
- 1 cup fresh spinach leaves
- 1/4 cup strawberries, sliced
- 1 tablespoon crumbled feta cheese
- 1 tablespoon chopped walnuts (or pecans)

Dressing:
- 1/2 tablespoon balsamic vinegar
- 1/2 tablespoon olive oil
- 1/2 teaspoon honey
- Salt and pepper to taste

Instructions:
1. Arrange the fresh spinach leaves on a plate.
2. Add the sliced strawberries and crumbled feta cheese on top of the spinach.
3. Sprinkle the chopped walnuts (or pecans) over the salad.
4. In a small bowl, whisk together balsamic vinegar, olive oil, honey, salt, and pepper until well combined.
5. Drizzle the dressing over the salad just before serving.
6. Toss lightly to combine and serve fresh.

Tropical Kale and Avocado Salad with Citrus Dressing

Time: 15 mins

Ingredients:
- 2 cups kale, stems removed and leaves chopped
- 1/2 ripe avocado, sliced
- 1/2 mango, cubed
- 1 tablespoon sliced almonds
- 1 tablespoon pumpkin seeds
- 1 tablespoon hemp seeds
- Lime slices, for garnish

Dressing:
- 2 tablespoons olive oil
- 1 tablespoon fresh lime juice
- 1 teaspoon honey
- Salt and pepper to taste

Instructions:
1. In a large bowl, massage the chopped kale with a pinch of salt until the leaves start to soften and wilt, about 2 minutes.
2. Add the cubed mango and sliced avocado to the bowl with kale.
3. In a dry pan over medium heat, lightly toast the sliced almonds and pumpkin seeds until golden and fragrant, then remove from heat.
4. Whisk together the olive oil, lime juice, and honey in a small bowl to create the dressing. Season with salt and pepper to taste.
5. Drizzle the dressing over the salad and toss gently to combine.
6. Sprinkle the toasted almonds, pumpkin seeds, and hemp seeds over the salad.
7. Garnish with lime slices.
8. Serve immediately and enjoy your refreshing Tropical Kale and Avocado Salad with Citrus Dressing!

Vietnamese Rice Noodles Salad with Sesame Dressing

Time: 25 mins

Ingredients:
- 1/4 cup cooked rice noodles
- 1/2 cup purple cabbage, shredded
- 1/2 carrot, julienned
- 1/4 red bell pepper, thinly sliced
- 1 tablespoon fresh cilantro, roughly chopped
- 1/2 teaspoon green onions, chopped
- 1/2 teaspoon sesame seeds

Dressing:
- 1/2 tablespoon sesame oil
- 1/4 teaspoon soy sauce
- 1/4 teaspoon rice vinegar
- 1/2 teaspoon honey
- 1/2 teaspoon grated ginger
- 1/2 clove garlic, minced
- 1/2 teaspoon sesame seeds
- Salt and pepper to taste

Instructions:
1. Prepare the rice noodles according to the package instructions, then cool under cold water and drain.
2. In a large bowl, combine the rice noodles, shredded purple cabbage, julienned carrot, and thinly sliced bell pepper.
3. In a small bowl, whisk together sesame oil, soy sauce, rice vinegar, honey, grated ginger, minced garlic, and sesame seeds to create the dressing.
4. Pour the dressing over the noodle mixture and toss to combine thoroughly.
5. Transfer the salad to a serving plate and garnish with chopped cilantro, green onions, and a sprinkle of sesame seeds.
6. Serve immediately or chill in the refrigerator before serving for a more refreshing taste.

Watermelon Salad with Feta and Mint

Time: 10 mins

Ingredients:
- 1/4 cup watermelon, cut into cubes
- 1/4 cucumber, sliced into half-moons
- 2 tablespoons feta cheese, crumbled
- Fresh mint leaves for garnish
- Salt to taste

Dressing:
- 1 tablespoon olive oil
- 1/2 tablespoon lime juice
- 1/2 teaspoon honey
- Salt and pepper to taste

Instructions:
1. In a serving bowl, combine the watermelon cubes and cucumber slices.
2. In a small bowl, whisk together olive oil, lime juice, honey, salt, and pepper to create the dressing.
3. Drizzle the dressing over the watermelon and cucumber.
4. Sprinkle crumbled feta cheese over the salad.
5. Garnish with fresh mint leaves.
6. Serve immediately or chill in the refrigerator for a short time before serving.

Roasted Butternut Squash with Feta and Red Onions

Time: 40 mins

Ingredients:
- 1/4 cup butternut squash, peeled and sliced
- 1/4 red onion, sliced into wedges
- 1 tablespoon feta cheese, crumbled
- 1 tablespoon olive oil
- 1/2 teaspoon za'atar spice mix
- Fresh watercress for garnish
- 1 tablespoon pumpkin seeds
- Salt and pepper to taste

Dressing:
- 2 tablespoons olive oil
- 1 tablespoon balsamic vinegar
- 1/2 teaspoon honey
- Salt and pepper to taste

Instructions:
1. Preheat your oven to 200°C (400°F).
2. In a large bowl, toss the butternut squash slices and red onion wedges with olive oil, za'atar, salt, and pepper.
3. Spread the seasoned squash and onion on a baking sheet in a single layer.
4. Roast in the preheated oven for 25 minutes or until the squash is tender and caramelized.
5. In a small bowl, whisk together olive oil, balsamic vinegar, honey, salt, and pepper to create the dressing.
6. Arrange the roasted squash and onion on a serving plate and drizzle with the dressing.
7. Garnish with fresh watercress and sprinkle pumpkin seeds over the top.
8. Serve warm or at room temperature.

Vegan Salads

Zesty Avocado Corn Salad

Time: 15 mins

Ingredients:
- 1 ripe avocado, diced
- 1/4 cup cherry tomatoes, halved
- 1/4 cup sweet corn kernels, cooked
- 1/2 cup cucumber, diced
- 1 tablespoon red onion, finely chopped
- A handful of fresh cilantro, chopped
- 1 jalapeño, seeded and finely chopped (optional)
- Salt and pepper to taste

Dressing:
- Juice of 1 lime
- 1 tablespoon olive oil
- 1/2 teaspoon agave syrup
- 1/2 teaspoon cumin powder
- A pinch of chili powder (optional)

Instructions:
1. In a large bowl, combine the diced avocados, halved cherry tomatoes, corn kernels, diced cucumber, and finely chopped red onion.
2. If you're using jalapeño, add it to the bowl for an extra kick.
3. In a small bowl, whisk together lime juice, olive oil, honey or agave syrup, cumin powder, chili powder (if using), salt, and pepper to create the dressing.
4. Pour the dressing over the salad and toss gently to coat the ingredients without breaking the avocado pieces.
5. Garnish with chopped cilantro.
6. Taste and adjust the seasoning if necessary.
7. Serve immediately or chill for a short time to let the flavors blend together.

Carrot and Cumin Salad

Time: 15 mins

Ingredients:
- 1 cup shredded carrots
- 2 tablespoons flat-leaf parsley, chopped
- 1 tablespoon almonds, slivered and toasted
- 1/2 teaspoon cumin seeds, toasted
- Lemon wedges for serving

Dressing:
- 1 tablespoon extra virgin olive oil
- 1/2 tablespoon lemon juice
- 1/2 teaspoon ground cumin
- Salt and pepper to taste

Instructions:
1. In a dry pan over medium heat, toast the cumin seeds and slivered almonds separately until they become aromatic and the almonds are golden brown. Remove from heat and allow to cool.
2. Peel and shred the carrots using a grater or food processor.
3. In a large bowl, combine the shredded carrots, toasted cumin seeds, and toasted almonds.
4. Chop the parsley and add it to the carrot mixture.
5. For the dressing, whisk together the olive oil, lemon juice, ground cumin, salt, and pepper in a small bowl.
6. Pour the dressing over the carrot mixture and toss well to coat.
7. Adjust the seasoning to your taste and serve the salad with lemon wedges on the side.
8. Enjoy this vibrant and crunchy salad as a healthy side dish or a light main course.

Falafel Salad with Hummus Dressing

Time: 30 mins

Ingredients:
- 3-4 falafel balls
- 1 cup mixed salad greens
- 1/2 cup cherry tomatoes, halved
- 1 tablespoon red onion, thinly sliced
- 1/2 cucumber, sliced
- 1/2 yellow bell pepper, diced
- 1 tablespoon crumbled feta cheese
- 1/2 tablespoon sesame seeds

Hummus Dressing:
- 3 tablespoons hummus
- 1 tablespoon olive oil
- 1 tablespoon lemon juice
- 1 teaspoon water (or as needed for consistency)
- Salt and pepper to taste

Instructions:
1. If the falafel balls aren't pre-cooked, cook them according to the package instructions or your recipe until they are crispy on the outside.
2. In a large bowl, combine the mixed salad greens, cherry tomatoes, sliced red onion, cucumber, and diced yellow bell pepper.
3. In a small bowl, whisk together the hummus, olive oil, lemon juice, and water until you reach a smooth, pourable consistency. Season with salt and pepper to taste.
4. Arrange the salad on a plate and distribute the falafel balls evenly on top.
5. Drizzle the hummus dressing over the salad.
6. Sprinkle crumbled feta cheese and sesame seeds over the salad.
7. Serve immediately, while the falafel is still warm.

French Beans with Hazelnut and Orange Salad

Time: 15 mins

Ingredients:
- 1 cup French beans, ends trimmed
- 1 orange, peeled and segments cut
- 1 tablespoon hazelnuts, toasted and roughly chopped
- 1 teaspoon orange zest
- Salt to taste
- Black pepper to taste

Dressing:
- 2 tablespoons extra virgin olive oil
- 1 tablespoon orange juice, freshly squeezed
- 1/2 teaspoon white wine vinegar
- 1/2 teaspoon Dijon mustard
- A pinch of sugar
- Salt and pepper to taste

Instructions:
1. Bring a pot of salted water to a boil and blanch the French beans for 2-3 minutes until they are bright green and tender-crisp.
2. Drain the beans and immediately plunge them into ice water to stop the cooking process and retain their color.
3. Once cooled, drain the beans and pat them dry with a towel.
4. Arrange the French beans on a serving plate.
5. Top with the orange segments and sprinkle with the toasted and chopped hazelnuts.
6. Grate some fresh orange zest over the salad for added flavor.
7. In a small bowl, whisk together the extra virgin olive oil, orange juice, white wine vinegar, Dijon mustard, a pinch of sugar, salt, and pepper until the dressing is well combined.
8. Drizzle the dressing over the salad just before serving.

Fresh Herb and Cucumber Salad with Crispy Pita

Time: 10 mins

Ingredients:
- 1/2 cup cucumber, diced
- 1/2 cup cherry tomatoes, halved
- 2 radishes, thinly sliced
- 1 tablespoon fresh parsley, roughly chopped
- 1 tablespoon fresh mint leaves
- 1 whole wheat pita bread, toasted and broken into pieces
- 1 tablespoon olive oil
- Salt to taste
- Black pepper to taste

Dressing:
- 2 teaspoons olive oil
- 1 teaspoon lemon juice
- 1/2 teaspoon dried mint
- Salt and pepper to taste

Instructions:
1. In a large mixing bowl, combine diced cucumber, halved cherry tomatoes, and thinly sliced radishes.
2. Add roughly chopped fresh parsley and mint leaves to the vegetables.
3. Drizzle 1 tablespoon of olive oil over the salad and season with salt and black pepper. Gently toss to combine.
4. In a small bowl, whisk together 2 teaspoons of olive oil, lemon juice, dried mint, salt, and pepper to create the dressing.
5. Drizzle the dressing over the salad and toss again to ensure all the ingredients are well coated.
6. Place the toasted pita pieces around the edge of the plate or mix into the salad for added crunch.
7. Serve immediately and enjoy your fresh herb and cucumber salad with crispy pita.

Garlicky Mushroom Buddha Bowl

Time: 30 mins

Ingredients:
- 1 cup cooked rice, cooled
- 1 cup mushrooms, sautéed in garlic
- 1/2 avocado, sliced
- 1/2 cup cherry tomatoes, halved
- 1 cup mixed salad greens
- 1 tablespoon chopped parsley
- Salt to taste
- Black pepper to taste

Dressing:
- 2 tablespoons tahini
- 1 tablespoon lemon juice
- 1 teaspoon maple syrup
- 1-2 tablespoons water (to thin)
- Salt to taste
- Black pepper to taste

Instructions:
1. Prepare the rice according to package instructions and allow it to cool.
2. Sauté the mushrooms in a pan with garlic until they are browned and fragrant.
3. Arrange the mixed salad greens in a bowl as the base.
4. Add the cooked rice to one side of the bowl on top of the greens.
5. Place the sautéed mushrooms next to the rice.
6. Add the sliced avocado and halved cherry tomatoes to the bowl.
7. Sprinkle the bowl with chopped parsley.
8. To make the dressing, whisk together tahini, lemon juice, maple syrup, water, salt, and black pepper in a bowl until smooth and pourable.
9. Drizzle the dressing over the Buddha bowl.
10. Season with additional salt and pepper if desired.

Grilled Courgette, Broad Beans, and Peas

Time: 20 mins

Ingredients:
- 1 medium courgette (zucchini), sliced lengthwise
- 1/2 cup broad beans, blanched and peeled
- 1/2 cup fresh peas, blanched
- 1/2 tablespoon olive oil
- 1 clove garlic, minced
- 1/2 fresh chili, finely sliced
- Salt to taste
- Black pepper to taste

Dressing:
- Lemon zest, for garnish (optional)
- 1/2 tablespoon olive oil
- Fresh mint leaves, for garnish
- Salt to taste
- Black pepper to taste

Instructions:
1. Prepare the rice according to package instructions and allow it to cool.
2. Sauté the mushrooms in a pan with garlic until they are browned and fragrant.
3. Arrange the mixed salad greens in a bowl as the base.
4. Add the cooked rice to one side of the bowl on top of the greens.
5. Place the sautéed mushrooms next to the rice.
6. Add the sliced avocado and halved cherry tomatoes to the bowl.
7. Sprinkle the bowl with chopped parsley.
8. To make the dressing, whisk together tahini, lemon juice, maple syrup, water, salt, and black pepper in a bowl until smooth and pourable.
9. Drizzle the dressing over the Buddha bowl.

Grilled Tofu and Avocado Salad Bowl

Time: 30 mins

Ingredients:
- 1/4 ripe avocado, sliced
- 1/4 cup cherry tomatoes, halved
- 1/4 cup black beans, rinsed and drained
- 1/4 cup corn kernels
- 1/4 block of firm tofu, cut into cubes and grilled
- 1/8 red onion, thinly sliced

Dressing:
- Fresh cilantro leaves for garnish
- Drizzle of creamy dressing (possibly a ranch or garlic aioli)
- Optional: sprinkle of black sesame seeds or nigella seeds on the avocado

Instructions:
1. Begin by pressing the tofu to remove excess moisture. Cut it into bite-sized cubes.
2. Season the tofu cubes with salt, pepper, and any other desired spices, then grill them until they have nice char marks and are heated through.
3. Arrange the grilled tofu, sliced avocado, halved cherry tomatoes, black beans, sliced red onions and corn kernels in separate sections for a visually appealing presentation.
4. Add the fresh cilantro leaves over the top.
5. Drizzle your choice of creamy dressing over the salad.

Hearty Kale and Baked Tofu Salad

Time: 30 mins

Ingredients:
- 1 cup kale, stems removed and leaves chopped
- 1/2 cup baked tofu, cubed
- 2 tablespoons red onion, thinly sliced
- 1 tablespoon sliced almonds, toasted
- Salt and pepper to taste

Dressing:
- 2 tablespoons tahini
- 1/2 tablespoon apple cider vinegar
- 1/2 tablespoon soy sauce
- 1/2 tablespoon maple syrup or honey
- 1 tablespoon water, to thin
- 1/2 small garlic clove, minced
- A pinch of smoked paprika (optional)

Instructions:
1. Preheat the oven to 400°F (200°C) and line a baking sheet with parchment paper.
2. Cut tofu into cubes, season with salt and pepper, and bake for 20-25 minutes until golden and crisp, turning halfway through baking.
3. While tofu is baking, prepare the dressing by whisking together tahini, apple cider vinegar, soy sauce, maple syrup, water, minced garlic, and smoked paprika if using until smooth.
4. Place the chopped kale in a large salad bowl and massage it with a small amount of the dressing to soften the leaves.
5. Once the tofu is baked, let it cool for a few minutes, then add it to the bowl with kale.
6. Add the sliced red onions and toasted sliced almonds to the salad.
7. Drizzle the rest of the dressing over the salad and toss to combine.

Italian-Style Vegan Chop Salad

Time: 15 mins

Ingredients:
- 1 cup chopped romaine lettuce
- 1/2 cup canned chickpeas, rinsed and drained
- 1/2 cup cherry tomatoes, halved
- 1/2 avocado, diced
- 1/2 cup diced cucumber
- 1/2 cup thinly sliced red onion
- 2 tablespoons chopped fresh basil

Dressing:
- 1 tablespoon olive oil
- 1/2 tablespoon red wine vinegar
- 1/2 teaspoon dried oregano
- Salt and pepper to taste

Instructions:
1. In a large salad bowl, combine the romaine lettuce, chickpeas, cherry tomatoes, avocado, cucumber, red onion, and fresh basil.
2. In a small bowl, whisk together the olive oil, red wine vinegar, dried oregano, salt, and pepper to create the dressing.
3. Pour the dressing over the salad and toss to combine, ensuring all the ingredients are evenly coated.
4. Serve immediately, or chill in the refrigerator for up to 1 hour to allow the flavors to blend.

Mediterranean Artichoke and Bean Salad

Time: 15 mins

Ingredients:
- 1 cup canned artichoke hearts, drained and quartered
- 1/2 cup green beans, trimmed and blanched
- 1/2 cup roasted red peppers, sliced
- 1 cup arugula leaves
- 1 tablespoon chopped fresh parsley

Dressing:
- 1 tablespoon extra virgin olive oil
- 1 tablespoon lemon juice
- 1 teaspoon Dijon mustard
- 1 small garlic clove, minced
- Salt and freshly ground black pepper to taste

Instructions:
1. In a mixing bowl, whisk together the olive oil, lemon juice, Dijon mustard, minced garlic, salt, and black pepper until the dressing is well emulsified.
2. In a salad bowl, combine the drained and quartered artichoke hearts, blanched green beans, and sliced roasted red peppers.
3. Pour the dressing over the salad ingredients and toss gently to coat everything evenly.
4. Add the arugula leaves and chopped parsley to the bowl, and give the salad another light toss.
5. Serve the salad immediately, or let it marinate for 10-15 minutes to allow the flavors to meld.

Mediterranean Butternut Squash with Pecans

Time: 45 mins

Ingredients:
- 1 cup butternut squash, peeled and cubed
- 1 tablespoon pecans, toasted
- 1 tablespoon olive oil
- 1 teaspoon honey
- 1/2 teaspoon cinnamon
- 1/2 teaspoon cumin
- Salt and pepper to taste
- Fresh herbs (such as thyme or parsley) for garnish

Dressing:
- 1 tablespoon balsamic vinegar
- 1 tablespoon extra virgin olive oil
- 1/2 teaspoon Dijon mustard
- 1/2 teaspoon maple syrup
- Salt and pepper to taste

Instructions:
1. Preheat your oven to 400°F (200°C). Line a baking sheet with parchment paper.
2. Toss the butternut squash cubes with olive oil, honey, cinnamon, cumin, salt, and pepper until evenly coated.
3. Spread the squash on the prepared baking sheet and roast for 30 minutes or until tender and slightly caramelized, stirring halfway through.
4. While the squash is roasting, toast the pecans in a dry pan over medium heat for 3-4 minutes.
5. For the dressing, whisk together balsamic vinegar, extra virgin olive oil, Dijon mustard, maple syrup, salt, and pepper in a small bowl.
6. Once the squash is done, allow it to cool slightly before transferring to a serving dish.
7. Drizzle the dressing over the warm squash and toss gently.
8. Top with toasted pecans and garnish with fresh herbs.

Mexican Corn and Quinoa Salad

Time: 35 mins

Ingredients:
- 1/2 cup cooked quinoa
- 1/2 cup sweet corn kernels
- 1/2 cup diced red bell pepper
- 1/2 cup diced green bell pepper
- 1 tablespoon finely chopped red onion
- 1 tablespoon chopped fresh cilantro
- 1 tablespoon olive oil
- Juice of 1/2 lime
- Salt and black pepper to taste

Dressing:
- 1 tablespoon olive oil
- Juice of 1/2 lime
- 1/2 teaspoon ground cumin
- Salt and pepper to taste

Instructions:
1. In a large bowl, combine cooked quinoa, corn, red bell pepper, green bell pepper, red onion, and cilantro.
2. In a small bowl, whisk together olive oil, lime juice, ground cumin, salt, and pepper to create the dressing.
3. Pour the dressing over the salad and toss to coat evenly.
4. Taste and adjust seasoning with salt and pepper if necessary.
5. Serve immediately, or refrigerate to let the flavors blend for about 30 minutes before serving.

Mexican Mixed Bean Salad

Time: 10 mins

Ingredients:
- 1/2 cup black beans, drained and rinsed
- 1/2 cup red kidney beans, drained and rinsed
- 1/2 cup sweet corn kernels
- 1/2 cup diced red onion
- 1/2 diced ripe avocado
- 1/2 cup cherry tomatoes, halved
- 1 tablespoon chopped fresh cilantro
- Salt and black pepper to taste

Dressing:
- 1 tablespoon olive oil
- 1/2 tablespoon lime juice
- 1/2 teaspoon chili powder
- 1/2 teaspoon garlic powder
- Salt and pepper to taste

Instructions:
1. In a large bowl, mix together the black beans, kidney beans, corn, red onion, cherry tomatoes, and cilantro.
2. In a small bowl, whisk together the olive oil, lime juice, chili powder, garlic powder, salt, and pepper to create the dressing.
3. Drizzle the dressing over the salad and toss gently to combine.
4. Top with diced avocado and gently mix.
5. Season with salt and pepper to taste.
6. Serve immediately or chill in the refrigerator for 30 minutes to allow flavors to meld.

Moroccan Cauliflower Salad with Pine Nuts

Time: 35 mins

Ingredients:
- 1 cup cauliflower florets
- 1 tablespoon olive oil
- 1/2 cup pine nuts
- 1/2 cup pomegranate seeds
- 1 tablespoon chopped fresh parsley
- Salt and black pepper to taste

Dressing:
- 1 tablespoon extra virgin olive oil
- 1/2 tablespoon lemon juice
- 1/2 teaspoon ground cumin
- 1/2 teaspoon paprika
- Salt and pepper to taste

Instructions:
1. Preheat the oven to 400°F (200°C).
2. Toss the cauliflower florets with olive oil, salt, and pepper, and spread them on a baking sheet.
3. Roast in the oven for 20-25 minutes or until the cauliflower is tender and the edges are golden brown.
4. While the cauliflower is roasting, toast the pine nuts in a dry pan over medium heat until they are golden, watching carefully to avoid burning.
5. In a small bowl, whisk together the extra virgin olive oil, lemon juice, ground cumin, paprika, salt, and pepper to create the dressing.
6. Once the cauliflower is done, transfer it to a serving bowl.
7. Drizzle the dressing over the cauliflower and toss to coat.
8. Sprinkle the toasted pine nuts and pomegranate seeds over the salad.
9. Garnish with chopped fresh parsley.

Panzanella Salad

Time: 30 mins

Ingredients:
- 1 cup stale bread, cut into 1-inch cubes
- 1/2 cup cherry tomatoes, halved
- 1/2 cup diced red onion
- 1/2 cup diced yellow bell pepper
- A pinch of torn fresh basil leaves
- Salt and black pepper to taste

Dressing:
- 1 tablespoon extra virgin olive oil
- 1/2 tablespoon red wine vinegar
- 1/2 teaspoon minced garlic
- Salt and pepper to taste

Instructions:
1. Preheat the oven to 375°F (190°C).
2. Spread the bread cubes on a baking sheet and drizzle with 1 tablespoon of olive oil; toss to coat.
3. Bake in the preheated oven until the bread cubes are golden and crisp, which should take about 10 minutes.
4. In a large bowl, combine the roasted bread cubes, cherry tomatoes, diced red onion, diced yellow bell pepper, and torn fresh basil leaves.
5. In a small bowl, whisk together the remaining olive oil, red wine vinegar, minced garlic, salt, and pepper to create the dressing.
6. Pour the dressing over the salad and toss to combine, ensuring that all the ingredients are well coated.
7. Let the salad sit for about 10 minutes before serving to allow the bread to absorb the flavors and become slightly softened.
8. Taste and season with additional salt and pepper if needed.

Pearl Barley and Roasted Red Pepper Salad

Time: 40 mins

Ingredients:
- 1 cup cooked pearl barley
- 1/2 cup roasted red peppers, sliced
- 1/2 cup cherry tomatoes, halved
- 1 tablespoon chopped fresh parsley
- Salt and black pepper to taste

Dressing:
- 1 tablespoon olive oil
- 1/2 tablespoon red wine vinegar
- 1/2 teaspoon Dijon mustard
- 1/2 teaspoon honey
- Salt and pepper to taste

Instructions:
1. Cook the pearl barley according to the package instructions, then allow it to cool.
2. In a salad bowl, combine the cooled pearl barley, sliced roasted red peppers, and halved cherry tomatoes.
3. In a small bowl, whisk together the olive oil, red wine vinegar, Dijon mustard, honey, salt, and black pepper to create the dressing.
4. Drizzle the dressing over the salad and toss to coat all the ingredients evenly.
5. Garnish the salad with the chopped fresh parsley for added flavor and freshness.
6. Taste and adjust the seasoning with additional salt and black pepper if necessary.
7. You can serve this Pearl Barley and Roasted Red Pepper Salad at either room temperature or chilled, depending on your preference.

Queen Buddha Bowl

Time: 50 mins

Ingredients:
- 1 cup cooked brown rice
- 2 tablespoons diced firm tofu, pan-fried until golden
- 2 tablespoons shredded red cabbage
- 1/2 avocado, sliced
- 2 tablespoons cubed mango
- 2 tablespoons cooked edamame beans
- 1/4 cup shredded carrots
- 1/2 tablespoon green onions, chopped
- 1/2 tablespoon sesame seeds

Dressing:
- 1 tablespoon tahini
- 1/2 teaspoon soy sauce
- 1/2 teaspoon maple syrup or honey
- 1/2 teaspoon rice vinegar
- 1/2 teaspoon sesame oil
- Water to thin, if necessary

Instructions:
1. Start by arranging the cooked brown rice as the base in a large bowl.
2. Next, place the pan-fried tofu, shredded red cabbage, sliced avocado, cubed mango, cooked edamame beans, and shredded carrots on top of the brown rice in separate sections.
3. Sprinkle the chopped green onions and sesame seeds evenly over the entire bowl for added flavor and texture.
4. In a small bowl, whisk together the tahini, soy sauce, maple syrup or honey, rice vinegar, and sesame oil until the dressing is smooth. You can add a little water to thin it out if needed to reach your desired consistency.
5. Drizzle the prepared dressing over the Queen Buddha Bowl, ensuring it's evenly distributed.
6. Mix the ingredients together before eating to combine all the flavors.

Spicy Tempeh and Asian Slaw Salad

Time: 50 mins

Ingredients:

For the Tempeh:
- 80g tempeh, cut into thick strips
- 1/2 tbsp soy sauce
- 1/2 tbsp maple syrup
- A pinch of garlic powder
- A pinch of smoked paprika
- 1 tsp olive oil

For the Slaw:
- 1/2 cup shredded purple cabbage
- 1/4 cup shredded carrots
- 1 tbsp chopped green onions
- A few cilantro leaves for garnish
- A sprinkle of sesame seeds

Dressing:
- 1 tbsp rice vinegar
- 1 tsp sesame oil
- 1/2 tbsp soy sauce
- 1/4 tsp ginger, grated
- 1/2 clove garlic, minced
- 1 tsp maple syrup

Instructions:

1. In a small bowl, combine the soy sauce, maple syrup, garlic powder, and smoked paprika. Add the tempeh strips for at least 15 mins.
2. Heat olive oil in a pan over medium heat. Once hot, add the marinated tempeh strips for 2-3 mins on each side.
3. In a mixing bowl, combine the shredded purple cabbage and shredded carrots for the slaw.
4. In a separate small bowl, prepare the dressing by whisking together the rice vinegar, sesame oil, soy sauce, grated ginger, minced garlic, and maple syrup.
5. Drizzle the dressing over the shredded cabbage and carrots. Toss the slaw well.
6. Place the dressed slaw on a serving plate and arrange the cooked tempeh strips on top.
7. Garnish the salad with chopped green onions, cilantro leaves, and a sprinkle of sesame seeds.

Turkish White Beans Salad

Time: 10 mins

Ingredients:
1/4 cup canned white beans, rinsed and drained
1/2 cup cherry tomatoes, halved

1/4 red onion, thinly sliced
1 tablespoon fresh parsley, chopped
1 tablespoon fresh mint, chopped
Salt and pepper to taste
Lemon wedges for serving

Dressing:
- 3 tablespoons olive oil
- 1 teaspoon lemon juice
- 1/2 teaspoon red wine vinegar
- 1/2 teaspoon honey
- 1/2 small garlic clove, minced
- Salt and pepper to taste

Instructions:
1. In a large bowl, combine the white beans, cherry tomatoes, and thinly sliced red onion.
2. In a small bowl, whisk together the olive oil, lemon juice, red wine vinegar, honey, minced garlic, salt, and pepper.
3. Pour the dressing over the white bean mixture in the large bowl. Gently toss the ingredients to ensure they are evenly coated with the dressing.
4. Add the chopped fresh parsley and fresh mint to the salad. Mix them into the salad.
5. Taste the salad and adjust the seasoning with additional salt and pepper if needed, according to your preferences.
6. To serve, provide lemon wedges on the side. Squeezing lemon juice over the salad just before eating adds a zesty and refreshing touch.

Healthy eating is happy living.

Made in the USA
Las Vegas, NV
23 April 2024